ACCLAIM FOR
DIVINE BREADCRUMBS

"Rachael Jayne Groover has an effortless ability to raise you up and move you forward with her words. This brave and generous account of loss, love, trauma, and triumph clarifies what it really means to surrender your life to a Higher Power, and at the same time, never give up on your bold and seemingly unrealistic dreams."

~ SUZANNE EVANS, NEW YORK TIMES BESTSELLING AUTHOR OF
THE WAY YOU DO ANYTHING IS THE WAY YOU DO EVERYTHING

"*Divine Breadcrumbs* is one of those few select books that takes you on a profound journey of the mind, soul and spirit. Rachael Jayne Groover's wisdom about how to be in flow with life rather than the struggle of life is both inspiring and activating. This amazingly fulfilling read is for those who are called to play a bigger game with their lives. I literally could not put it down once I started. It is now on all my clients 'must read' list."

~ RICK TAMLYN, HAY HOUSE INTERNATIONAL AUTHOR OF
PLAY YOUR BIGGER GAME

"For anyone seeking a relationship that is supportive, passionate, fun, and lasting, *Divine Breadcrumbs* is a must-read. Through her heart-ache and humiliation in love Rachael Jayne Groover shares with humor and wisdom what it really takes to become a person who is truly ready for an extra-ordinary relationship."

~ JANET MCGEEVER, BEST-SELLING AUTHOR OF
TANTRIC SEX AND MENOPAUSE

"An uplifting and provocative read. *Divine Breadcrumbs* has inspired me even more to pay attention to my inner voice, intuitive hits, and heart's desires. They are the signs leading us all to an abundant and meaningful life. Rachael Jayne Groover is a powerful storyteller, shining the light on her global leadership abilities in the art of personal and spiritual transformation. This book will inspire many to dream big."

~ GENA DAVIS, BEST-SELLING AUTHOR OF
YOGAMASS: EMBODYING CHRIST CONSCIOUSNESS

"Rachael Jayne Groover is one of the smartest and most insightful business people I've ever met. *Divine Breadcrumbs* will make you wonder, allow you to dream, and at times make you laugh out loud—all the while helping you to realize and manifest your incredible human potential. She has a beautiful way of reminding us that all our journeys are unique and spiritual in their own way."

~ DEL LEWIS, SERIAL ENTREPRENEUR,
FOUNDER AND CEO OF TRICLARE BUSINESS HOLDINGS

"*Divine Breadcrumbs* drew me in deep. I couldn't put it down. Rachael Jayne Groover's story is an exhilarating and emotional ride. It made me cry, laugh, root for her, and want to steal her courage. The surprises were endless. In the end, the biggest surprise was what it revealed about my own journey of hope, never giving up, and trusting in my Higher Power."

~ LISA JACKSON, CEO,
CORPORATE CULTURE PROS

DIVINE
BREADCRUMBS

A SEARCH FOR TRUE LOVE AND ENLIGHTENMENT

BY

RACHAEL JAYNE GROOVER

DEEP PACIFIC PRESS

Fort Collins, Colorado, USA

DIVINE
BREADCRUMBS

A SEARCH FOR TRUE LOVE AND ENLIGHTENMENT

BY

RACHAEL JAYNE GROOVER

Deep Pacific Press
117 E. 37ᵗʰ Street #580
Loveland, CO 80538
http://DeepPacificPress.com

Divine Breadcrumbs / Rachael Jayne Groover - 1st ed.
ISBN 978-0-9832689-2-5 (paperback)

Cover Design: Tenth Muse Design
Cover Photography: Don Hajicek

Books and Programs by Rachael Jayne Groover

BOOKS

Powerful and Feminine:
*How to Increase your Magnetic Presence
and Attract the Attention You Want*

PROGRAMS

Art of Feminine Presence®
ArtofFemininePresence.com

Awaken Your Impact®
AwakenYourImpact.com

The Awakened Speaker™
TheAwakenedSpeaker.com

Meet Rachael Jayne Groover online and receive free training at
RachaelJayne.com

• DEDICATED •

to my sister,

AMY KENNEDY

Thank you for having the courage to follow

your Divine Breadcrumbs

into uncertain territory and an inspiring career.

• CONTENTS •

THE GREATEST BATTLE

There is a way between voice and presence
where information flows. In disciplined silence it
opens.
With wandering talk it closes.

~ **RUMI**

The most important battle of our lives is the one going on inside us.

On one side is the voice of love, potential, possibilities, and unlimited solutions to what we see as a problem.

On the other side is the voice of fear, limitations, restrictions, and ego patterns, which are the constant creators of our so-called "problems."

These voices give us directions constantly.

The answer to eradicate all our physical, emotional, mental, financial, and relationship pain lies within the question: *Which voice will I listen to?*

I'm strategic. I'm a hard worker. I'm practical. But not until I wrote this book and looked back on the most painful and thrilling times in my life did I realize how these traits were hindering me—possibly more than they were helping.

When I first felt the call to write this book, I allowed my logical mind to take the lead, and it came up with these questions:

1. What topics should I follow on from my first book, *Powerful and Feminine?*
2. What topics would expand the audience that I had already reached with my seminars?
3. What topics would sell the most copies?
4. What topics would get the attention of a top literary agent and subsequently a publishing deal?

I decided to first work out what makes logical sense, and then I could add my creativity and my heart. After all, others in my fields of spiritual coaching, healing, and personal development have a lot of heart but not the strategies to make a profitable business work.

One day during morning meditation I heard a clear voice say, "This book should not be written from your strategic mind." I enjoyed feeling that loving presence sweep through me, and I knew it spoke truth. It was exciting. However, the burst of passion waned when I remembered that I wanted this book to become a bestseller.

You have to use your left brain to make that happen, I told myself. *This has to be marketable. You have more to lose now because business is booming. You have a brand, an office, and a staff to keep going.*

With those two voices competing for attention, I chose to focus on my deepest desire, which was to allow Grace to write this book through me. I wanted to get my limited mind out of the way and write what flowed. I wanted that for my life as well. I surrendered to a new way of writing and prepared to live in an open and curious state.

I meditated a lot. I practiced free writing while feeling connected to my more expanded voice. Dates finally lined up within my busy work schedule to write the book. In Sedona, Arizona, on August 25, 2016, the entire first draft was written in 22 hours of writing over 2½ days. In stillness, a powerful voice recalling long-forgotten, life-altering memories came through.

It had never occurred to me beforehand that I would write an account of my spiritual awakening, of my embarrassing love life, and of the Grace that guided me and opened doors I never could have opened myself. I thought I would write a self-help book on conscious feminine leadership, or something like *17 Ways to Make a Bigger Impact in the World.* That is what I teach, so that would be a natural choice.

Grace had something else in store for me—again. It took me on another path—again. It led me to a better, more exciting, and more infinite place—again.

This is not the self-help book my left brain had planned to write. This is a more personal book. I have been led back to a truth that is vibrantly important for me: true love, joy, loyalty, career fulfillment, and abundance are not always found in the people and/or places we think. However, they are always present if we let our Higher Power lead—and if we have the guts to follow.

I invite you now into my story—raw and uninterrupted. A story remains the most powerful way to learn and remember what your Soul is trying to tell you. Let it affect you as it is meant to. Let it remind you of what you need to remember. Join with me to contemplate what could happen if you slowed down long enough to see your next Divine Breadcrumb—and are trusting enough to pick it up.

CHAPTER 1

UNNATURAL HABITAT

"I don't want to go home," Satina declared.

I sighed. "I know. I don't want to either."

Going home to Australia would mean nothing had changed. Going back would mean a return to the status quo. Going back would mean we'd no longer be seen as unique or exotic. Everyone we'd met in the USA loved Aussies. Especially since it'd only been a year since the world fell in love with us while watching the 2000 Sydney Olympics. We were novel and had sexy accents.

Satina and I both secretly craved to be seen as different. We *were* different. But most people in Australia didn't understand us because we didn't fit in with the current Aussie culture. We were often judged for being enamored with all things metaphysical while we judged them for floating down the mainstream river, drowning their dreams one beer at a time.

Satina and I sat by the window of a local restaurant and watched with delight the unfamiliar sight of moist snow gently falling on the sidewalk and slowly melting on windscreens of parked cars. The dark vinyl of the American diner booth under our butts and the famous brands of condiments we'd never seen in real life set dead center on the distressed wood table were enough to make us giddy. We reminisced about the past six days and how this was a divinely inspired trip. Twenty-four hours earlier we'd finished our first *Conversations with God* retreat in Ashland, Oregon, with best-selling author Neale Donald Walsch. We didn't meet him personally, but it didn't matter— our lives had changed. The retreat was emotional, mind-altering, and full of people we could relate to. Little did I know where it would take us.

It was only a few months after September 11—a very tense time to be traveling in the United States, but we didn't care.

"We knew we were meant to be here, didn't we? We always have to follow our knowing," Satina said with an undertone of begging me to stay with her as a friend on a path less traveled.

I was willing to follow her anywhere. I wanted excitement. I had attended the retreat because of Satina. We met after she found a posting I'd made online about a spiritual circle I led in Melbourne—my hometown in Australia. Barely five foot two, she was the most elegant woman I'd ever met. She had an intensity and outspoken nature that I was drawn to and repelled by at the same time. She turned up one night to our circle and had us spellbound with her energy and by the way she talked about her worldly past and spiritual understanding. A few months later, when she spontaneously asked me to travel to America and attend the *Conversations with God* retreat with her,

I knew I had to go. This didn't make logical sense, as I had just emptied all my savings on my first trip to the States five months earlier. I was living month-to-month as a singer, teaching voice and musical performance on the side. Spare money was always elusive. I heard I could receive a scholarship for the retreat, but I still had to find $2,000 for a plane ticket from Melbourne to Medford, Oregon. I had no room on my credit cards—just an intense compulsion to go.

At the same time the university where I was finishing my music business degree announced a singing competition. They wanted someone to sing the national anthem and another song specifically written for that year's graduation ceremony. The prize was an opportunity to sing in front of an audience of 40,000 people—and $2,000. I knew entering was a long shot, since dozens of qualified singers had applied. No one was as surprised as me that I won.

For the first time I sensed a presence on my side that was helping me get to America. I booked my plane ticket, withstood a grueling 17 hours in a center seat of the economy cabin and was sitting in the third row of the retreat two weeks later.

"I feel I am meant to stay here for another month. There is more here for me," Satina announced.
Satina was usually the first to say things aloud. She had the self-confidence I wanted.

"I feel the same way," I replied with excitement.

Our mantra since we'd met had been, "Follow what we know we're meant to do." By the time our pumpkin pie had reached the table for dessert, we'd agreed to extend our plane tickets by 30 days. Yet somehow, we had to conjure up a miracle and find a place to stay. Neither of us could afford to live a month at our current hotel. I'd used up a year's worth of vacation money during my past week there. We declared we would "put it out to the Universe" and hope an opportunity would show up. We had no idea how it was going to happen, though we had faith it would.

We didn't know anyone in town except a few people on the Conversations with God staff and a few locals who attended the retreat, but within two days a house dropped in our laps. A couple who had been at the retreat heard we were open to house-sitting. That fit their plans perfectly, for they were leaving town for three weeks. We moved in two days later. We took a day to adjust, nap, and dream about our upcoming month—which would start with an informal gathering that night.

Satina and I were both too responsible to hold any wild parties in a house that wasn't our own, especially one with a white picket fence, gigantic oak tree in the front yard, and a porch swing that made us smile.

We had become friends with a fellow retreat participant named Cedric who'd flown over from Switzerland. Cedric was super smart, spoke four languages, was very talkative, a little nerdy (in an adorable way), and looked like an Italian version of Clark Kent—glasses and all. We invited him to stay with us for a few nights, as there were plenty of rooms. Satina had made friends with a local couple, Tom and Susan, who were in their mid-forties and who were obviously in love and very sweet.

They were invited over that night too, along with David, an acquaintance of Cedric's.

As David walked in the door, his soft white body told us he didn't see the sun much and didn't know what exercise was. His unkempt brown beard told me he didn't have a girlfriend, either.

"Hi, I'm David. I heard you had a wonderful time at the retreat with Neale," he said in a voice that was a cross between a radio announcer and someone trying way too hard to sound wise and spiritual. He leaned in and jolted me with a hug that lasted 45 seconds as he placed one hand on my tailbone and one hand on the back of my heart. I didn't know whether to laugh, scream, or slap him. Was this an American thing? He finally released me from his grip, and before moving to Satina to repeat the exact same ritual he looked deeply into my left eye, as if staring into that particular eye long enough—in that specific way—would eventually open me up to see the depth of his spiritual and sexual prowess. I thought he was creepy, but no one else seemed to mind. Everyone looked up to him because he was a trusted member of Neale's staff.

We snacked on dips, crackers, and falafel balls around the coffee table, leaned back on the couch, and talked about spirituality, Ashland, and Neale—whom everyone there seemed to accept as their guru. At the end of the night David led us in a meditation that the others happily followed along with. I still could not get past his creepiness—of him, his voice, and now this weirdo meditation he was having us do. I started to feel sick to my stomach, and for a moment I was scared to stay in the house with these people.

The scared little girl inside me had her first freak-out of the trip.

How well do you know these people? You don't even know Satina very well, a voice inside me said. I calmed that voice down by excusing myself when Tom and Susan left for the night. I was tired, but mainly I wanted to get away from the weird energy and have some much-needed alone time. I've always been an introvert and need more alone time than most. I've always had a bit of a split personality, where I will be super shy and hermit-like, and then change on a dime to be the life of the party. Mostly I like being the hermit. I've gone weeks without seeing or talking to anyone and loved every moment. I fell asleep that night to the background sound of David, Cedric, and Satina in deep conversation and laughter.

I woke up and groaned almost immediately as I heard David's voice coming from the kitchen. He'd slept over and was now talking to Cedric over the occasional clang of a frying pan and utensil. How long could I read, curled up under the feather comforter before needing to go to the bathroom? *A long time*, my little girl said.

Suddenly, I heard a strange sound. It was a mix between a cry, a scream, and a yelp. Within seconds, Cedric banged on my bedroom door. "Satina is yelling for you. She's in the shower and needs you now! Something's wrong."

I jumped into my tracksuit pants and hooded sports top as fast as I could. As I sprinted up the staircase that led to the master bedroom, her anguished cry grew louder. Cedric and David were right behind me. I opened the door, took a few steps into the bedroom, and got my first glimpse of Satina in trouble. In the bathroom Satina was standing naked in the tile shower, water running over her head, her body shaking with both arms stretched out to her side. I froze.

Cedric quickly strode forward and turned off the water. The two men carried her out of the shower and into the bedroom.

"Satina! Are you okay?" Cedric said, trying to snap her out of her catatonic state. "Satina, what's happening? Talk to us," he pleaded.

She did not look like she heard him. Her eyes were rolled back in her head, and she shook like a possessed woman in a horror film.

"She's not okay, guys. She's not okay," I kept repeating in a tense voice. "Should we call an ambulance?"

"No!" Satina's immediate and emphatic response shot out with more of the personality I was used to. She looked me square in the eye and said, "I'm okay. I'm coming back to the room now."

The three of us stood around her in silence, breathing heavily, waiting for her to speak again. Then her body started convulsing again. This time the shaking became more forceful.

"What is happening?" I said, terrified.

Satina's tiny body was still naked and sweating from the heat of the shower. Each time we tried to cover her, she ordered us not to. She started moving in wavelike undulations in the middle of the king-size bed. David acted like he'd seen this a million times and could take care of it. He placed his hands under her back as an attempt to calm her down. Cedric was trying to figure out what would keep her safe. Should we go against her wishes and call an ambulance? I was freaked out and no help to anyone.

After another five minutes Satina started to calm down, and eventually her body became completely still. She looked at me standing across the room—the friend that she had brought across the Pacific Ocean on this crazy adventure. She could see I was terrified. "Sweetheart, come and lie beside me here. It's okay. I'm okay." She patted her hand on the bed next to her.

Cedric tried to cover her body with a blanket.

"Don't cover me. I'm still heating up. Please, just come and lie beside me."

I crawled onto the bed but didn't get too close. I should have been comforting her, but she was the one comforting me. She explained the experience that she'd just had. "Something took me out of my body in the shower. It's happened before. I got scared that I would not be able to get back in. That's why I started yelling for you, sweetie. It was the most beautiful thing. I just got scared."

If that is what a magnificent spiritual experience looks like, I don't want any part of it, I thought. Cedric and David lay on the bed with us. We listened to Satina talk. We eventually all fell silent. God knows what the guys were thinking. I couldn't help taking an outside look at myself and thinking, *If only my beer-drinking musician friends could see me now.*

CHAPTER 2

THE SOOTHING
STRANGER

I was concerned that some weird, psychic, unusually dark energy had come into the house the night before. I felt terrible there. I couldn't comprehend what was going on, and the sickness in my stomach that started when David walked into the house was constantly roiling. To my relief, David finally had to leave for work. Satina, Cedric, and I spent the entire day processing what had happened. Even though Satina seemed at peace with it, I was exhausted, upset, and scared. I wanted to go home. I didn't want to be around these people anymore, but with no car and lots of snow I was stuck. A naive, sheltered Australian girl was not meant to have these sorts of experiences, I thought. Early that evening I told Satina how afraid I was. She listened to me with the love of an unconditional older sister and allowed me to vent without her adding any unwanted advice. I drenched a few tissues and felt some relief.

"I don't want to stay at home tonight. I need to get out of this house," I told her.

"Where do you want to go?"

"I want to go to a bar and dance and get rid of this heaviness. You keep telling me I have to follow what I know how to do. Well, what I know is I want to get the hell out of here and have a drink."

"Then let's go," Satina said with a cheeky smile. "I want to do whatever will make you feel better."

I have never been a big drinker, but that night I anticipated how sublime a couple glasses of wine would feel after the day I just had.

We invited Tom and Susan out with us, and they picked us up in their four-wheel drive. Along with Cedric and a friend of Tom's, we ended up at the Ashland Springs Hotel bar, where we knew a band was playing. I'd told Satina that David was not welcome, but to keep that to herself. I was a chronic people pleaser, so even though he repulsed me, I didn't want him to hear about it and make him feel unwanted.

When we arrived at the hotel it was loud, dark, and packed full of locals. My tension level immediately dropped. Bars like this were like home to me. I was usually in the band watching people trying their best dance moves. The loudness of the music and people shouting to be heard made me feel serene. The packed-in nature of the crowd made me feel held. The smell of alcohol inspired me to take a deeper breath.

Our posse had to walk in single file to wind through the crowd enough to see where we might perch ourselves. I couldn't see who was leading, but I was the last of our group. The cry from my heart was: *I just want to be led tonight. I want to be shown where to go next. I want to get out of my head and relax for a while.*

The person in the lead found one remaining table at the back of the room, farthest from the band and the bar. Our conga line veered off to the left. As I reached the bottom of the three steps up to where they were headed, I felt an invisible hand gently but firmly stop me and a confident voice inside my head say, "Don't go that way. Do not sit with them. Go sit at the bar."

What? I wondered who was talking to me.

The inner voice repeated the instructions again. "Don't go that way. Do not sit with them. Go sit at the bar."

The message was so strong, I grabbed Satina's shoulder in front of me and said, "I'm being guided to go sit at the bar."

Anyone else might have thought I was crazy, but she just winked and said, "Have fun."

Before my left brain kicked in, I walked back through the crowd and found a way to the bar. The beat of the band got louder. There were no bar stools left and only one narrow space to stand between two people, so I took it. I turned to the handsome bald guy next to me who seemed like he was on his own too, and half-heartedly said, "Hi."

His smile was warm as he introduced himself. "Hi, I'm Robert."

"I'm Rachael Jayne."

"How are you?" he asked with a hundred times' greater sincerity than I'd ever experienced from a man at a bar before.

"Do you want the truth or the superficial answer?" I asked.

"The truth, of course. Why anything else?"

"It's been an intense day, but I'm feeling better now. Thanks for asking."

"Is that an Aussie or Kiwi accent I hear?"

"Aussie."

I felt comfortable talking to him but nervous at the same time. I turned to the wall of liquor and mirrors behind the bar for help.

"Can I buy you a drink?"

"That would be lovely."

A mojito seemed like an appropriate choice. As I sipped the sugar and licked the salt, he shared the details of his life with me—what he did for work and how long he'd lived in the area. I noticed no wedding ring. I shared what had brought me to Ashland, and he'd heard of Neale. After only one drink I found myself telling him what I'd sworn I wouldn't say. I hadn't yet figured out if my habit of telling too much too quickly was a good or bad personality trait. One part of me couldn't believe I was telling this stranger at a bar about Satina's out-of-body experience and my freak-out, and the other part of me drank in his caring ear and masculine presence like I had not had any water for days.

He leaned in as I told him everything. He was genuine as he said, "What a day. I appreciate you trusting me enough to share that."

"I bet you think I am crazy now," I announced in an attempt to lighten the mood.

"Not at all," he replied.

Robert was a welcome surprise. He was sensitive but not a New Age kind of guy. He listened as much as he talked—and it didn't hurt that he was cute. He had the closest shave on his head possible and blue eyes that seemed to take up half his face. He looked like a tall, 40-year-old cross between Sting and Ed Harris.

When I saw my friends jiving on the dance floor, it ignited a desire to join them. He wasn't up for dancing. He motioned to the dance floor with his head. "You go ahead. I'm not going anywhere."

After taking a few minutes to break into a sweat with my mates, I looked back at this man I had opened up to, and he was entirely focused on me. I didn't break our eye contact until it sent a flutter through my heart and a zing down my core. *Oh yikes,* I thought. I'm always great with guys until I really like them. Then I suck at this game.

For all 26 years of my life I'd never had a real boyfriend. I had one for two weeks when I was eighteen, but he only kissed me twice. Then he admitted he was gay, so that really doesn't count on the scorecard. I was a great flirt. I showed sexy bravado on the outside but felt awkward on the inside. I was a hopeless romantic who yearned for a deep, passionate love affair with a soul mate, so not attracting a single man who would want to date me was painful and embarrassing. Everyone else I knew had experienced a relationship with at least one boyfriend or girlfriend. What was wrong with me? Insensitive so-called friends would ask that sometimes. It was humiliating.

Robert didn't move until I returned to his side. "You're a great dancer," he offered as he leaned in closer. This time the light press of his shoulder against mine felt sensual. "I know you have your friends here, but if you ever feel like you want to get out of the house, I can show you some beautiful parts of this area. I work for myself, so I can be flexible during the daytime." He handed me his business card. "Call me anytime, but only if it feels right."

I could feel both the lack of attachment and desire that came with his proposal. He changed my mood that night—more than the alcohol. No man had ever listened to me with such intensity. His eyes empathized and his smile soothed me to safety. I took his number. I was the one who couldn't stop shaking that night.

CHAPTER 3

STAR MAKER

I've secretly wanted to be a star since I was seven. I wanted to perform to large crowds and make people feel something deep. I loved the idea of having a spotlight on me. When I first heard about the Star Maker competition, well before my visions for living in the USA had started to bloom, I vowed to do everything I could to win it. I performed most of the time in bars and at weddings because that is where the secure money was. The genre for my original tunes was a variant of country music, and that was what I saw as my ticket to fame. I followed the path of many country music hopefuls, which was entering as many talent quests as possible so I would be "discovered." In Australia, Star Maker was the most prestigious contest of all. The winner was essentially guaranteed to be one of the most famous names in Australian country music because of the record deal, prize money, and the national tour they'd be sent on after they won.

I'd tried to get accepted into the Star Maker final for three consecutive years. To be chosen as one of the twenty finalists, you had to submit a recording of your music plus a written application of why you would be a great representative for the establishment known as Country Music Australia. After two years of not making it in, the third year I opened their acceptance letter with a set of instructions. It was a great lesson to not give up and to allow myself time to earn the right to play with the big guns. I'd been like many people—impatient, expecting my success to be handed to me without putting in the time to become good enough to be accepted. Finally, I was in the running.

In January 2001, I made the 12-hour drive to Tamworth, Australia, in a caravan of two minivans with seven girlfriends and seven family members in tow. My family had come to cheer me on and my girlfriends to drink, dress up, and hopefully kiss a cowboy or two. They were a big attraction for big-city girls who rarely stepped out of Melbourne.

Diane Kennedy, my mum, was my biggest fan and the only one in the caravan of groupies who liked traditional Australian country music. She was a "child whisperer"—at the schools where she taught and at home. Her four children were given equal amounts of love and discipline. We were offered praise to grow and criticism to improve. She never told us our homework was fantastic when it wasn't. She never said, "You are awesome!" She showed us her feelings of pride and support by her actions.

She and Dad had backed my first CD project, City Girls, which got me to the Tamworth finals. Boxes of unsold copies of it gathered dust under their bed for years. They didn't care. They were proud, and I knew it.

I was prepared and hopeful. It was an amazing experience to sing for 3,000 people on a scorching summer day in an air-conditioned auditorium. The wood floors and massive sound system made it a singer's paradise. The perfectly lit stage made us all look like superstars. I was elated when I advanced to become one of ten in the final round. I knew I had an excellent chance to win after seeing everyone perform earlier that day. My 14-member fan club thought only a few were in my league.

That evening, each grand finalist sang three songs for a televised national audience. Earlier that day, all ten of us had been interviewed as part of the selection process because the country music establishment had to approve the person who would essentially represent them for the next year as the up-and-coming Star. Every industry has their "establishment" that runs most of what goes on behind the scenes, and I met them that afternoon.

After the final performance, I knew I was one of two who rose above the rest. I knew I had a solid shot at winning. For the next year of my life I would be recording my second album and constantly traveling, singing in clubs and hotels, entertaining country folk. I was a city gal at heart. Even though my edgier style of dress and music were more progressive than most Australian country music audiences liked, I could see myself as a country star. It's what I had trained for and focused on for years.

During the afternoon, my family, friends, and I concluded that the winner was going to be me or the cute, tassel-wearing, guitar-playing Kylie Sackley. With no time to go anywhere, we hung out in the foyer of the historic building, gazing at the legends of Australian country music on the walls while trying to tame the butterflies in our stomachs.

As the announcement over the loudspeaker came for the contestants to convene backstage, Mum pulled me aside. "We will be proud of you no matter what happens tonight, and we will always know the truth. The truth is, you were the best up there." I knew she was biased, but the support felt great.

I experienced a heavenly moment on stage that night. I was born to be in the spotlight. I knew it without a doubt, even though I did not have the guts to say that aloud for several years.

As I sat back in the front row with heavy makeup, wearing a red faux-leather skirt and black sequined halter top, I started praying. My prayer consumed all my attention, which seemed weird given the venue. It was as if my prayer had the spotlight trained on it, not the final contestant on stage. This particular prayer had been a constant refrain over the last month, but as the announcement of the winner drew nearer, it gained greater focus. The prayer was not a prayer to win. It was a prayer for my highest good. It was a prayer to have the outcome of this competition lead me to my soul's purpose. I wasn't 100% happy about this prayer flooding into my attention. I wanted to win. I had spent over $10,000 in singing lessons and thousands of hours in practice time. I was meant to be a star, and this was my best shot at it.

In primary school I had learned all the Catholic sacraments, and I became a leader in our Christian youth group during the last years of high school. As much as I believed Jesus' teachings would help guide my mission in life, I thought a lot of what the church preached was outdated and chauvinistic. I had many an argument with fathers of my friends who thought the Catholic church was justified in not allowing women to be priests, despite the fact that almost all of the other Christian denominations were already allowing them. During high school my mum also started to think that the church's rituals were irrelevant, which she didn't dare tell her church friends. She'd always been an open-minded thinker, not taking anything or anyone at face value.

"I cannot reconcile in my heart that just because they were born in India or China, they are not going to heaven because they don't believe in Jesus Christ," she said one day. That only made me respect her more.

Since high school I have had a passion for spirituality in all forms and traditions, and I deeply believe in a God-like presence in my life that is infinitely intelligent. I am comfortable calling that presence by different names: God, Grace, or Higher Power.

As I waited for the decision of who would win Star Maker, the words took over my mind with a gentle force: "If I am to win and that is how I can best serve, have me win. If this is not in my highest interest, there must be something else even better for me."

No, no, no…I want to win, the other part of me said, holding on to control.

Right before they were ready to announce the winner, I chose to give up control. The pull to listen to my Higher voice was strong. I started chanting to myself, "Guide me, protect me, and I will follow through." Even with the massive gold letters STAR MAKER on the stage banner broadcasting potential fame, I started to feel unattached, even though this was a prize I had wanted for a very long time.

Before that night I'd never fully relinquished my life to my Higher Power. The thought of letting go of control was too unsettling. My limited mind had resisted with the same mantra: *You need to have a plan and never quit.*

Becoming a country music star was my plan.

I theoretically knew that following my Higher Power could lead to unlimited possibilities and those spontaneous meetings with others in the right place at the right time. Nonetheless, in the past I'd cut the connection through doubt, worry, and fear. I thought I had to keep rigid control because if you don't worry enough about what you want, it won't happen on its own. I told friends, "I have to worry about this because if I don't, who else will? I want to make sure what I want actually happens."

I was changing my tune. I was singing a new song. I was scared, but I wanted to take an exhilarating ride, not one that was just full of entertaining drunk people in bars or at parties and weddings.

"And the winner is Kylie Sackley."

My heart sank as I struggled to be at peace with the decision. It helped my ego afterward to hear from one of the judges how he thought I should have won (he had drunk one too many beers that night and shouldn't have been telling me that), but I felt I was on the verge of an important turning point in my life.

Only a few weeks later I decided to travel to America for the first time. I could feel its magnetic pull. I felt the draw to live there, to experience the music there, to experience the men there, and the spiritual teachers that seemed plentiful there. I took losing the competition as a sign to make room to travel to America versus traveling around Australia entertaining country folks with my new country songs. At the time I didn't comprehend just how much Grace had stepped in. There was no victory, no fame, and no kissing of cowboys. I drove back to Melbourne with a feeling in my heart that my failure was somehow meant to happen and was making room for something else.

• CHAPTER 4 •

KEITH URBAN
AND THE U.S. OF A.

My love affair with America started years before my first trip there, ignited by my love for American country music. The good stuff, not what you hear on mainstream country FM stations. Yes, I am a music snob. I was a schizophrenic snob when I studied music at college. My alter ego would love to channel the angst of Alanis Morrisette, Nikka Costa, and any woman artist who had the ovaries to use profanity in their lyrics, but I would eventually be drawn back to the wholesome, politically correct lyrics of country. My tastes mirrored my personality. I wished I could be the bad girl, but I really wasn't.

I learned to play acoustic guitar, keyboard, and electronic drums, but voice was my main instrument. The dusty back corners of my family cupboards still have the VHS tapes from when I was eight that prove I always loved to perform. I embody more of the performer archetype than a singer or musician. It's the feedback loop with the audience that turns me on. I communicate with them and they communicate with me. They feel me—and I feel them. I've never been one of those musicians who would play or practice much between gigs. But I loved those gigs.

What I love about quality American country music is the storytelling. Lyle Lovett, Bonnie Raitt, Reba McEntire, Allison Krauss and Union Station, EmmyLou Harris, Willie Nelson, Johnny Cash, Dolly Parton, Lucinda Williams, Trisha Yearwood, and Vince Gill—all of those voices, among others, make something move inside of me. I want to be told a story. American country music told of places and people I wanted to meet. I liked the simplicity of the music, as long as it wasn't too simple. It made me cry, it made me feel love, and it made me feel okay with my loneliness. I still tear up every time I hear Trisha Yearwood sing that last verse of "She's in Love with the Boy." She sings, "Katie looks at Tommy like I still look at you," and the waterworks turn on. Call me a hopeless romantic.

At the time Australia did not have a huge country music scene, and much of it was not to my taste at all. When I heard good American country music I felt home, but traditional Australian country music left me bored. It was just too daggy for me. Keith Urban was a whole other story, however. I saw him perform while I was in Tamworth for Star Maker. He'd been living in the States for nine years on his quest to become a star. He'd just released a new album that was getting air play, and he was becoming well-known there after many years of toughing it out. I got to witness the magic, the chops, and the sexiness that is Keith Urban that night. It only made me want to go to America more. Amid the fumes of beer and cigarettes in that half-filled room I realized he was indeed one of the best guitar players of our time, and as I danced ten feet from his golden hair and sweaty, tattooed body, I knew he was a kindred spirit. Call it fantasy or connection. After that night I said to myself, "I'm like Keith Urban. I am as cool as Keith Urban. I am too cool to stay in the Aussie country music scene. They just don't get me here." Looking back, I realize I was crazy. No one walking this planet is as cool as Keith Urban.

I started to seriously consider how I was going to become a star over there like my bro Keith. I had the huge atlas in the family home office permanently opened to the two-page spread of the United States. I would look at it almost every day and wonder, *Where should I live? How could I manage to stay there and work permanently?* On all accounts, people told me that it was practically impossible at my age. Unless you had a master's degree and experience in an industry for which they needed people—or a million dollars to sink into their economy—it was almost impossible to get a work visa. As a singer who had quit college twice, was teaching kids and adults to sing, and was performing in bars at night, I was not the model of what the United States was looking for. But I felt there had to be a way.

I looked at cities I'd heard of like Memphis, Nashville, Birmingham, Waco, and Lubbock. I idealized how cool these cities must be to live in. I would dream about being a teacher at a community college. I could get my visa by teaching during the day and sing my heart out at night.

Every time I looked at the atlas, the feeling that my true love lived in the United States grew stronger. That insight—or fantasy—added fuel to the fire, and my attachment to making the move burned out of control. I'd tell myself that I had to go, and I would do whatever it took to live there. I wasn't willing to miss out on love anymore. I became excited when I studied the map and started dreaming. On the other hand, I felt a little desperate at how mundane most of my days had become. I told my closest friends, "The love of my life is living in America. I don't know how I know that, I just do."

I could feel his love calling me from across the largest and deepest ocean in the world. On happy days I stared at the atlas, staying open to where I'd be led. On melancholic days I would be overwhelmed with the cold reality that finding my soulmate in a country of over 300 million people would be like finding a needle in a haystack.

No matter what my mood was, on every morning walk I'd repeat my devotional statement: "Guide me, protect me, and I will follow through," saying it over and over at least 30 minutes a day. "Guide me, protect me, and I will follow through." Yes, I can get obsessed when I want something. I wanted change. I wanted adventure. I wanted true love.

One month after Star Maker, I started to plan my first trip to the USA, convinced I had to meet someone at an organization who would sponsor me for a visa. I laugh at my naivete now. I actually thought that I could fly solo to the other side of the world without knowing a soul, rock up to a few community colleges, and make such good friends with someone in one meeting that they would want to plow through weeks of paperwork and fees to hire me rather than an American citizen who needed the job.

I felt I had one shot at it, as it would take at least half a decade on my low income to save up money for a second trip. I planned to take a four-week trip across America, going to the cities that were my best educated guess of where I wanted to live and where my man might be. After deeper investigation on Waco and Lubbock, I learned the definition of the word "redneck." Instead, I chose San Francisco, Austin, Chicago, Nashville, and New York as my target cities. All my life I had lived in one of the most multicultural cities in the world, Melbourne, thriving with the sprawl of four million people. I didn't think I could survive in a small town without all the art, music, and culture bigger cities have to offer.

I landed in San Francisco alone, exhausted, and dreaming of a bed and blackout curtains after almost an entire day spent in the air. The problem was, it was ten in the morning and my hotel couldn't check me in until three. At least I could clean my teeth and pull my greasy hair back in the lobby restroom. They could store my luggage while I did some bleary-eyed exploring. I could only afford two nights at a hotel for my four-week trip, so I chose for them to be my first two nights. That way I could get over the jetlag before staying in youth hostels for the rest of my zigzag across the country. With pink Nikes on my feet, back-pack on my back, and money bag strapped to my waist under my clothes, I headed out to see the quintessential San Fran sights.

I reached the first crosswalk and stopped cold. I looked for a pedestrian signal, but there wasn't one. Cars raced by in either direction. I saw lines painted on the roadway that might have been for pedestrians to cross, but I didn't know for sure and with no button to initiate the traffic lights to stop the cars, I wasn't moving. Minutes passed. The day suddenly felt ten degrees hotter. I was overloaded with new sensory input: cars driving on the wrong side of the street, horns beeping, and road signs that didn't make sense. I hadn't even walked one block without getting stuck in this foreign land. Finally, a woman passed me and lunged out in the oncoming traffic. Miraculously, the cars stopped. I quickly jumped in behind her and made note of what pedestrian crossing markings looked like. I got to the end of the road and looked at my map, which told me I needed to turn right to walk down Mission Street.

I saw a sight I'd never witnessed before. A string of homeless on both sides of the street, lying or sitting on crushed cardboard boxes or old winter jackets. Most were visibly intoxicated. It was a shock to my innocent, sheltered eyes. As I passed a few side streets and found myself ogled by dirty-clothed men, all I wanted to do was turn around and retreat to the corner of that hotel lobby and sleep, but my ego kicked in and I kept walking. It would be way too uncool to give up on my first day of exploration. I took one step after another and ignored everyone who asked me for money or tried to talk to me.

Within ten minutes of touring the frantic San Francisco streets, I was freaked out. Why was I thinking that I could do this trip alone? I did my best to stay safe in the city until I returned to the hotel and checked in. It took me fifteen minutes to figure out how to turn the shower faucet on. Then I watched some disturbing news on NBC and cried myself into a sound twelve-hour sleep.

I had set up a meeting with John, the coordinator of the music department at one of the Bay Area's community colleges, for the next day. John and his wife took me out to dinner and showed me the most beautiful parts of the city. I now realized why people had said, "You'll love San Fran." John said he'd let me know if any music teaching position opened up, but his offer was lukewarm. Days later, during my stay at a hostel that overlooked the bay and the Golden Gate Bridge—with its views of Alcatraz, the Pier, and tourist walks—I just wanted to move on.

I traveled to Austin the following week and found relief immediately. Not from the heat—it was July and the most humidity I'd ever had to bear, but from the homeless and feeling anxious. I stayed at a hostel on Lake Austin and made a few friends my age. I thought it was funny—each morning I'd pass an American in the common area and they'd say *Howdy* and I'd say *G'day*. I spent most nights listening to world-class music that emanated from almost every bar and club. I loved staring at the unfamiliar sights of colorful murals on brick walls, the Texas flag that seemed to fly everywhere, and the long dreadlocks on men. I could see myself living in this music-centric town, but the meeting I had set up with the music coordinator at a local community college fell through the day before we were supposed to meet. I had no work prospects there.

In Chicago I found some stabilization. I stayed with Darren and Kim, friends from Melbourne who were now living there, which made me feel safe. I loved exploring the downtown area, the architecture, the bridges, and waterways from Lake Michigan, but found no job openings there either.

Nashville, the home of country music, was heaven to me. I felt like I was in a movie. I listened to a pedal steel guitar, fiddle, and dobro combination at the Grand Ole Opry. I went to the famous Songbird Café twice to watch the songwriters in the round. I sipped lemonade in twelve music venues in six days. I made some contacts with high schools and community colleges there, but I was so sidetracked by all the music that I wanted to see, I put aside trying to find someone to sponsor me. I started to feel I was on a wild goose chase with this job hunt, so I gave it up and became engrossed in listening to live music and dreaming of becoming a star. Yet soon I had to leave because my time was up. I had a plane ticket to New York I'd already booked before I hit the USA.

New York City in July scared the shit out of me. The city brought me to tears every day.

Day 1. I had my first panic attack ever—on a bus. I realized two minutes into the ride that I was on the wrong bus. My mind shut down. I didn't know which bus was the right one. As I looked around and saw every ethnicity represented, I didn't know who to ask or who I could trust. I started sweating and blushing and shouted to the driver, "I have to get off; I don't know where I am." A middle-aged Jewish woman took pity on me and got off the bus with me to help. I tried unsuccessfully to hold back my tears with this kind stranger as we held the map together.

Day 2. I was overwhelmed while finding myself on a fairly deserted street trying to make my way over to the UN headquarters. I'd heard all the news reports that had made their way Down Under about New York's crime rate. Now they were making me paranoid. *Am I safe? Who's behind me? Is someone going to stab me?* I vowed not to watch any more news reports on my trip.

Day 3. I didn't realize at first what I was looking at as I walked down 42nd Street—until I got close enough to see that it was some old guy's hairy butt as he was pissing into the gutter. That was it! I locked myself in my tiny hostel room for two days while trying to drown out the constant bleat of car horns bleeding through the ancient single-pane window. I didn't talk to anyone. I was a scared bunny rabbit who would hurry out of its burrow for some New York–style pizza when hungry and run back as quickly as it could.

That trip taught me I wasn't as mature as I'd thought. Nor was I as confident and independent. On the final day of that first solo voyage to the USA, I plucked myself out of my top bunk and went to Ellis Island to see the Statue of Liberty. I had to have photos of it to show people when I went home. It was a perfect weather day. Clear skies, calm breeze, scenic boat ride, and great history tour. Before heading back for the return trip to

Melbourne, I took some time alone on the manicured lawn and looked across at the stunning view of Manhattan, with the Twin Towers in the foreground. I found a peace I hadn't felt in days and wondered if I would ever see that particular sight again.

Given the emotional roller coaster of the trip, I was surprised when I realized so soon after my return flight that I still had the fixed resolve to move to America. I just had nowhere to move to and no money for another visit. I hadn't met anyone who wanted me, nor had I found a place I wanted to live. I'd returned home with my tail between my legs, needing to rest and regroup. I didn't tell anyone what a scared rabbit I'd been for most of the trip. When they asked me how it was, I showed them photos of famous landmarks and lied to their trusting faces, "It was amazing!"

• CHAPTER 5 •

AN UNDENIABLE MATRIX

My morning routine began again. My daily walk still included the prayer, "Guide me, protect me, and I will follow through." I added what I was grateful for and visualized how I wanted the day to unfold.

Over the past few years I'd been reading personal development books that helped me see what I could create in my life, but my real introduction to an expanded understanding of spirituality came through television.

A few years earlier, I'd cut my university classes to watch *Oprah* almost every Thursday. She started inviting spiritual teachers like Gary Zukav, Iyanla Vanzant, and Carolyn Myss as guests on that day. I was riveted. The desire to move to where all these cool personal growth-orientated people and spiritual authors lived grabbed me every time her closing credits hit the screen.

I remember being particularly drawn to Gary Zukav. I hung on his every word as he talked about his book *The Seat of the Soul*. He spoke with an understated presence that captivated me. He was my favorite "Thursday guru." I read his book five times in one year, marked it up with my lead pencil, and it became my bible. With each page I awakened to what the purpose of life was and my role in it.

Looking back, I see that my search for enlightenment started early. At age fifteen I was chosen for a leadership conference that was filled with personal development experiences. I loved every minute of it. At sixteen, I had loads of ideas on how to motivate my Catholic youth group to expand its views and make a positive impact on its members.

At age eighteen, I saw an advertisement on television featuring a bald, ginger-bearded man named Michael Domeyko Rowland. He looked out from the TV screen and asked, "Do you ever wonder why you have created the life you have created? Do you wonder about the meaning of life and how you can live your soul's purpose?" I crawled across the lounge-room carpet on my hands and knees to get closer to him. In a near-hypnotic trance I said, "Yes, I do, ginger-bearded man. I ask those questions all the time." I'd just found my first guru.

My next guru was Tony Robbins, whom I also found on TV. I scrounged up the $249 to buy his Personal Power 2 series on cassette tapes after watching the infomercial several dozen times as I partook in my after-dinner snack consisting of all major three food groups: chocolate, Doritos, and Coca-Cola. It didn't take a genius to work out why I was stacking on pounds per month. Tony's encouragement got me off the couch, off the Doritos, and to drop 40 pounds off my pudgy body. I developed a disciplined practice of creating my life the way I wanted it. From then I went through Tony's 30-day Personal Power program every year. I can see now how it made me think and act differently to my peers, who were more interested in dancing late at night, drinking beer, and making small talk. For much of my late teens and early twenties I felt insecure, as I thought others must perceive me as boring. Yet my internal landscape was anything but boring.

I kept being drawn back to the soft-spoken Gary Zukav, who I heard lived in Ashland, Oregon, a place I had not heard of before. My best friend Fiona and I would always joke about who we found more attractive—Dr. Phil McGraw or Gary Zukav. Even though Dr. Phil was younger, taller, and had more sexy, masculine energy, we both had a crush on Gary. I found out via his website that anyone could start a Soul Circle, which was a peer-led group of people wanting to gather to talk about the principles from *Seat of the Soul*. I discovered someone online who already had started a circle, so I joined their group of two. Shortly, we became a healthy group of five who read a new self-help book every month. Then one night we were visited by the mysterious Satina. I didn't know at the time how much everything would change as a result.

After a few weeks of Satina joining us, she boldly suggested we go away for a few days and have a retreat together.

We all loved the idea. Satina offered her beautiful, large home in Bendigo, in central Victoria. "It's the perfect place. I can send my husband and kids away for the weekend, and there will be a bedroom for everyone," she announced proudly. A few weeks before the retreat, I started feeling that something significant would happen there, but I had no clue what. As I finished packing my suitcase the night before, I heard a voice whisper a clear and specific instruction: "Take one of Amy's vases to the retreat." It was a strange request, and the voice repeated it a few times. "Take one of Amy's vases to the retreat."

My younger sister Amy had just started her career in ceramic arts. She'd decided to quit her university studies, which had brought her no joy but plenty of stress. She instead devoted herself to something people around her thought could never become a financially sustainable career. Anxiety about the decision enveloped her, but she decided to go for it.

I assumed that the request to bring the vase must mean that I was to give it to Satina as a gift for hosting us. I giftwrapped it and wrote a thank-you card.

I was given the bedroom at the farthest end of the house. I placed my suitcase on the bed and zipped it open. As I started unpacking, a book on the side table grabbed my attention. It was *Conversations with God—Book One*. I had only heard of it once before. I read the first page and then another. Before another item was unpacked, I was engrossed. I devoured the entire book in the three days.

I felt the nourishment of the first days of the retreat deeply. The six seekers present were all women who loved the time to share, read, and inquire into each other's limiting beliefs and discuss spiritual principles. *I could do this every week,* I thought on more than one occasion. One of the principles we kept coming back to was the idea that we have to take action on what we "feel called" to do. If we don't act on an inspiration that comes to us, resistance kicks in and we don't do something that needs to happen for us and others. By the same token, when we do something we know we are not meant to do, it also stops the flow and causes resistance. It all made perfect sense—right down to my soul.

On the evening before the final day of our retreat, I climbed under the bedcovers, and while meditating for a few minutes, I heard another clear voice say, "Don't give the vase to Satina—give it to Julie."

What? I didn't understand. I wasn't accustomed to hearing these voices.

I heard it repeat the exact same words: "Don't give the vase to Satina—give it to Julie."

Most of the women in the circle were 10 or more years senior to me, and I felt anxious about this message. What if there was no special reason to give this to Julie? What if it looked like I was trying to be something I am not? That would be so embarrassing. Plus, I felt I had to give something to Satina. I hadn't brought anything else for her. All these good reasons to not follow the guidance flooded in. I didn't want to risk speaking up. I had been burned several times when I shared something intuitive, and it was met by my peer group talking behind my back about how "up myself" I was. I feared this would happen again. The voice said for the third time, "Do not give that vase to Satina—give it to Julie."

"Okay, I got the message," I whispered back to God-knows-who.

Given the light of the principles we had considered over the past few days, I had no choice but to follow the advice of this voice.

I woke the next morning with the same message ringing in my ears. I already had experienced messages that told me, "Say something to this person" or "Do you really want to do that?" But this was different. I felt the clarity of the message keenly in both my mind and my body. I walked into the final session with the vase wrapped up in navy blue tissue paper and a white bow and not the faintest idea why I needed to give it to Julie.

It took the entire morning session for me find the courage to nervously speak up. I looked at Satina and Julie and forced my-self to declare in a trembling voice, "Before I came here I was given instructions by some 'higher knowing' to bring this gift with me. I thought it was for Satina. Last night the same voice said, 'Do not give this gift to Satina—give it to Julie.'"

I handed it to her with a confused look on my face. Satina smiled, proud of me for speaking up. She was becoming my mentor. I embraced that and trusted her. As Julie undid the bow that held the wrapping neatly around the gift, I started to tell her about the vase.

"My sister made it. She's just recently made the courageous decision to change careers and go for a career as an artist. Amy was scared to make the leap. I am so proud of her. Her pieces are already selling."

As the words came out of my mouth, tears welled up in Julie's eyes. I didn't know why, but I kept talking about Amy's decision to choose her art over security. She looked like she couldn't believe what I was telling her, and she pulled a tissue from the box on the coffee table.

I fell silent at last. Julie took a few deep breaths and explained, "I've been debating giving up my job to do my art full-time."

Goose bumps appeared on my arms. Now I needed a tissue. Julie continued. "My husband is not fully supportive of my plan because he's concerned about where the money would come from. I don't think I have the courage to do this without his support."

Now everyone needed tissues. Julie cried because of the sign that she had received. I cried because of what had happened when I trusted an inner voice even though I was worried about being humiliated. I almost didn't give the vase to Julie—and so this moment never would have happened. I wondered how many times I had not done something I should have in the past because of fear. The rest of the group was moved because what they had witnessed reminded them of how our lives are all woven together. We felt our bonds grow stronger.

At lunch, I sat across from Satina and apologized. "I now have nothing to give you as a gift, but I am so grateful that you opened your home to all of us."

The smile on her face penetrated my heart with such love that I couldn't control myself. I don't remember the exact words she spoke after that, but I will never forget the experience. I entered an altered state of reality right there at the dinner table, over pumpkin risotto and Parmesan cheese. I saw her influence in my life. I saw how I had drawn close to this woman for a special purpose. We had come together to do something amazing, and this was only the beginning. I could feel the presence of my Higher Power everywhere. I felt my heart burst open. With tears streaming down my face, I felt ecstasy. I didn't know what was happening. Satina looked back at me with tears in her eyes and a recognition of the altered state I was entering. She whispered, "This is where the power is."

I eventually got up from the table only to see two of the women on the sofa, having an argument. In my ecstasy I somehow saw the entire history of their lives and why in that moment they came together to create that argument. I looked around the room and saw the other two women talking. They were eliciting from each other what they had set in motion with their thoughts for most of their life. Everyone was creating their current reality in entirety, and the others interacting with them were the cooperative components to their creation. I not only felt how we are all part of an interconnected matrix, at that moment I could physically see it with my own eyes.

Satina had been walking a few steps behind me as I felt a deep desire to lay my eyes on everything. The other women eventually realized something unusual was happening to me because of the blissful look while tears ran down my face. They gathered around me and began talking, but as Satina raised her forefinger to her mouth, they fell silent. I understood much later that crying is an act of letting go of resistance so we can move up the emotional scale to feel better, whether we feel sad and need to release, or feel happy and cannot open to a higher form of love and joy.

Tears gushed from my eyes, soaking the collar of my shirt. Cleaning up my mess was the furthest thing from my mind as my body attempted to open to the pure bliss and ecstatic currents that had taken me over like a full-body orgasm created in union with the most perfect of lovers.

The mysterious presence that the poet Rumi often spoke of was with me as I wept, opening my mind and heart, seeing things as I had never seen them before.

> *I am so small I can barely be seen.*
> *How can this great love be inside me?*
> *Look at your eyes. They are so small,*
> *but they see enormous things.*

My state of expanded consciousness and bliss lasted for two weeks, and for another few weeks after that I experienced a powerful high where I'd never felt so full of possibility and happiness. During that time Satina learned about a retreat that Gary Zukav was leading in Ashland, Oregon, and had bought a ticket to go. I thought that was so cool. I could never afford to do something like that and couldn't wait to hear about her experiences when she returned.

A few weeks later, she heard that it had been canceled but still felt called to go to Ashland and have a spiritual adventure. With some online investigation she found an alternative. At our next Soul Circle gathering, she sat inches from me on the couch as she announced she wasn't going to see Gary anymore and had found out that Neale Donald Walsch, the author of *Conversations with God*, was holding a retreat at the same time, also in Ashland.

She turned to me and with those wise and mischievous eyes said, "Do you want to come with me?" She nodded slowly and confidently, as if the decision had already been made. "I think you're supposed to come with me."

CHAPTER 6

PRIMAL AND SPIRITUAL

Two days after meeting Robert at the Ashland bar, I worked up the nerve to pick up the phone to call him. I had checked him out online to see if his business card was legit, and he was not a psychopath. Before my fingers could dial the first number, I hung up the phone and stared at it. Willing myself to be courageous, I picked it up again. I put it down in seconds. I picked it up. I put it down.

I finally pulled myself together enough to follow through. When I heard his voice on the other end of the line, I was transported back to the crowd of dancers, the mojito, and the fullness of his lips. I thought, *I'll never get sick of hearing the American accent. It sounds so sexy on a man.* With my heart pounding fast, I asked, "Does your offer still stand? I'd love to hang out sometime."

"Yes, of course." He sounded pleased. "What would you like to see?"

I fortunately didn't verbalize the first answer that came to mind: *Your hot body.* Instead I said, "I'm open to whatever you have in mind."

"Would you like to have dinner tomorrow night and we could talk about options?"

"Sounds perfect."

After he inquired into how things were at the house since Satina's out-of-body experience a few days prior, we made plans for the following night to meet at the English pub in town, The Black Sheep.

Cedric had bought a rust bucket of a car for $300 from someone he'd just met, and he dropped me off at the pub. As I opened the creaky car door to get out, I gave him Robert's address and phone number and half-jokingly said, "If I'm not home when you wake up, call the police."

Alone and nervous, I climbed the dimly lit old wooden staircase in high-heeled boots that were almost as loud as the sound I was sure my heart was making. The owners had tried to create an English pub feel with Guinness on tap and soccer jerseys on the wall, but the place was huge, and with its high ceilings it was a far cry from the quaint pubs in London. As soon as the maître d' welcomed me, I saw Robert sitting very tall and straight at a table across the restaurant floor. My whole body became charged—not in an overtly sexual way, but in a way that said, "Pay attention; this is someone important."

I had previously experienced those vibrations in my body when first meeting someone who would end up making a difference in my life. Since reading my first spiritual books, I'd been trying to read the signs and pay attention to people who had been put in my path for a reason. I believed I was being led and felt like the lead actress in a movie. The "Divine flow" was happening to me—or through me. When I was in the flow and something extraordinary was about to shift my life, the sign almost always was a trembling of my body.

He stood up as I approached. He gave me a polite, short hug and pulled out my chair. As I took in the sight of him again, I felt validated that I was not imagining the connection we'd had the other night. Robert was masculine, present, sexy. He ordered some drinks, and as the bartender left, he asked me again how the last few days had been. I had to lean closer, as his voice was soft and more tender than I expected given his muscular physique. I assured him I felt a lot better.

"How has your week been?" I asked in the most confidently feminine tone I could produce.

"Good," he replied with a smile. "It's been hard not to keep thinking about our meeting the other night."

He had revealed more than I was prepared for, and I blurted out, "Me too," before I could censor myself.

I tried to converse like a normal person on a normal first date, but there was nothing normal going on there. With every minute that passed we felt a force drawing us together. It felt spiritual and sexual at the same time. It was as if all the other patrons and waiters and drinks in mid-pour had stopped, and there was nothing animated but us. In the long spaces of silence, we couldn't take our eyes off each other. It was uncomfortable, but it was the only thing we could do. We both imagined hearing an internal voice saying, "Pay attention to this person. This is a soul connection."

My appetite was gone. My senses were heightened to a level ten. I couldn't string an intelligent sentence together. I didn't know what was happening; I just knew that it was happening to him too. We made it only through the first round of drinks before he admitted that the energy between us left him with completely no appetite. I confessed to the same thing. He brought out the honesty in me too easily for my comfort zone.

"Do you want to get out of here and go somewhere we can really talk?" he asked.

We drove to his charming cottage home. It was clean and classy. Everything had its place. Every book fell in perfect unison with each other on the bookshelf, as I noticed we had similar tastes in spirituality, psychology, and art. He had nature photography on the walls, all held in white minimalist frames. He was a photographer and graphic designer, and his creative eye was evident throughout the house.

Though the rational part of me said I was crazy to go home with some guy I hardly knew, I was completely at ease. With a touch of a button, Alison Krauss and Union Station played the most masterful yet subtle bluegrass I had ever heard. With a flick of a switch, the perfect mood was set through subdued lighting. With the addition of some pinot noir into my glass, my heart rate increased.

This was always the moment when I tensed up and became more of a little girl than a woman. I became scared that a man would find out I wasn't as sexy as I came off earlier. I wouldn't know what to say. I unconsciously turned them off and I didn't know why. Alison Krauss might save me this time, I thought. If I could just focus on her sultry voice and the sensuality of the Dobro, that might do it.

He moved in to kiss me for the first time, and for me it was nothing short of a transcendental experience. His touch was soft and firm. The energy was both primal and spiritual. I felt transported to another realm. I had never experienced this before. On his ivory couch and sage cushions, we got lost in each other for hours without taking off anything more than our shoes.

He called the next morning to propose dinner at his place that night. We met at the local co-op, bought some ingredients, and walked the ten minutes back to his cottage. He loved to cook. I'd never had a man I liked cook for me before. He already knew I was vegetarian, so he was making one of his specialties: teriyaki tofu and kale over brown rice. As he chopped in his small, quaint kitchen, I sat on the couch, sipping a glass of wine, taking in every contour of his body.

"How was your day?" I asked.

Instead of answering my question, he laid his eyes on me for what seemed like an eternity of silence and said, "You look so good in my home."

I had never been on the receiving end of such a comment. I averted my eyes and sank deeper into my feminine essence as I let this man lead the evening.

Is this really happening? Is this what falling in love feels like? I was embarrassed to admit that I didn't know. I was so inexperienced in love. So familiar with my longing and unfamiliar with a man's loving attention.

He was the first to say that he loved me. I was the first to say I wanted to stay. We were so caught up in each other during that first week together that it hadn't fully registered that I was leaving Ashland in less than three weeks and I lived on the other side of the world. This was the first romantic love I'd ever experienced. I wasn't going to let the vast Pacific Ocean get in my way. I knew my ideal man lived in America. I just never thought I'd meet him so fast, in this divinely led way, with a guiding voice saying, "Go sit at the bar. Go sit at the bar."

He was an introvert like me. We didn't need to speak all the time. Silence between us was easy. He was more private and wasn't forthcoming with his history at times. I had to dig for the stories. He was twelve years older, and he stretched for half an hour a day on his yoga mat, which he said was the most important way to stay young. He looked at least ten years younger. He was also a gentleman. I had noticed in general how American males were more gentlemanly than the average Australian macho guy. I liked that—a lot.

The worry over my staying in-country kicked in. To live in Ashland with Robert, I had to find a way to get someone to sponsor me for a work visa.

Satina loved hearing about the unfolding romance, and she was ready to help when I asked, "Who will sponsor me? Can you help me brainstorm?" I didn't want to include Robert at that point, since I didn't want him to feel pressured to make a commitment so soon. I assured him I would only move there if I wanted to, regardless of what happened between us.

The same answer simultaneously came to Satina and me. The Conversations with God Foundation had a volunteer program.

"Do you know how it works?" I asked Satina.

"Yes. They pay a small stipend and give you a room in their volunteer house if you volunteer for 30 hours a week. You have to commit for at least six months. I already know they have an opening, as Cedric was investigating if he could stay and work for them for a while."

The next day, I marched across town in my winter gear, visualizing the way I wanted the meeting to unfold with Amy Anderson, the volunteer coordinator. I chanted my incantation in a steady beat all the way there, "Guide me, protect me, and I will follow through." I had rehearsed in my head why it would be in their best interest to hire me as their next volunteer. More to the point, why they should sponsor me for a visa so I could return and work legally. I don't think anyone at the foundation was in their right mind when they agreed. It made no sense for them to choose me because of the amount of extra paperwork and legal steps they had to take to ensure my immigration status. The effort would take them weeks. I had zero administration or customer service experience. I was a country singer. But I had already learned about myself that when I wanted something to happen, I was going to do anything I possibly could.

Not only was this visa a ticket into the country I had dreamed about for years, but it was also my ticket to love.

Satina decided she was not going home after our thirty days was up. She left with Cedric on a trip to see where she was led. This meant I had nowhere to stay for the final week. Without hesitation, Robert said, "Stay with me, silly. I see you every day anyhow."

Given my almost guaranteed return to the USA, our parting at the airport was not devastating. I would finalize the paperwork for my visa back in Australia so I could re-enter the States and start my new life in Ashland with this beautiful man. From what we knew about timelines of getting visas approved, I'd return in less than four months. When I said the words "four months" aloud, it felt like an eternity. After we had our last long kiss goodbye, he put his nose on mine and said, "Be patient. I'll be here when you get back."

• CHAPTER 7 •

LOVESICK

I'd always excelled in academics and sports. In other areas, I expected things would never work out for me. My love life was one of them. I had learned that lesson all the way through school.

In primary school I was shyer than almost every other girl and would never talk to boys if I didn't have to. I had a crush on a cute, tanned, brown-haired little boy every other girl liked—Cameron Buckley. He won our hearts because he possessed the unusual combination of being both popular and well-mannered. I never shared with anyone that I liked him. That would have been far too embarrassing.

In my transition to high school, I knew I had to make a drastic change. I got the clear cultural message that if I didn't change my ways, I would suffer years of being neglected.
Sitting in the front row of my year seven classroom, I paid close attention to the blackboard and received pats on the back from the teachers, but no second looks from boys. That was enough to

spark my reinvention. I chose the end-of-year holidays to make the switch. On the first day of year eight I immediately took the back-row seat next to the class bad boy, who was already making trouble with his friend on the other side of him. I had raised my uniform hem three inches and I'd dyed my hair bright burgundy. When the sun shone, it turned neon. I was the first to dye their hair, and I loved it when Mrs. Braithwaite, the most conservative of the Catholic teachers at school, approached me in the school yard. "Your hair color is not acceptable under the uniform policy, and you are wearing too much makeup for your age. How does your mother feel about this dreadful color of your hair?"

"She's fine with it," I replied. "She helped me dye it."

"You should be ashamed of the way you look. I don't know what has come over you, young lady," she said in her scratchy old voice.

I never wanted to be the bad girl. I was ashamed when I occasionally got in trouble. But I had never received this much attention, which I not only enjoyed, I wanted more of. I also wanted to entertain. I found that if I could make the teacher laugh, especially at the time they should have been reprimanding me, I hit the jackpot. I wanted the whole classroom to look at me as the most unique, quirky, and funny kid in the class. Hopefully, a cute boy would then take more notice. At least that was the plan.

"Why do you have that umbrella up inside, young lady?" Mrs. Potts said as she turned around from the blackboard she was writing equations on. All the kids in unison turned around to see me at my desk holding a fully opened umbrella above my head.

"Because it just started raining, Miss," I replied matter-of-factly.

The kids' laughter was music to my ears.

"Put that umbrella down now."

"But I might get wet, Miss!" I answered, trying not to giggle. The smiles on my classmates' faces were delicious to the performer in me.

"You will be sent out of the classroom if you do not put that umbrella down right now."

"Well, I think you need to send me outside, because I really don't want to get wet and I will if I put this umbrella down."

"Out!" Mrs. Potts said, pointing to the door as her patience disappeared.

I headed out the door, which was exactly where I wanted to end up. I had just seen one of the boys I had a crush on get kicked out of his class. I always chose a seat so I could easily see into the concrete courtyard in the middle of all of portable buildings that housed our year level. Even though I couldn't talk to him because of the twenty-five meters that separated us, at least he would see me get kicked out and know I was not a Miss Perfect, A-student, boring girl. Instead he would regard me as an exciting, wild teen who was potential girlfriend material. He looked over as the classroom door slammed behind me and gave me a small smile. That was enough. All year I found various ways to get kicked out of class. Just enough to get attention and not too much to have the teacher hate me.

By the end of year eight, I went boy crazy. I had crushes on so many of them that I started giving all twenty-eight of them numbers. I told only my most trusted girlfriends a few of the numbers so they knew it was a real system. I would talk about all of the most popular boys by substituting their name with their number so no one knew who I was talking about. I thought I was brilliant. I'm sure that wasn't the consensus from my peers, however.

As word of my weird system spread, all the boys wanted to know if they had a number and which one they were. It was a reason for them to approach me, which never happened in any previous school year. I wouldn't tell any of them their number, but instead I used the interaction to do my best job of flirting with them. I would have been happy if any of the twenty-eight asked me out—just once—or even flirted back with me, but none of them did. I watched them start pairing off with the prettier or more popular girls. I was neither. Boys thought I was smart, funny, and approachable, but they didn't put me in the category I wanted. Even with my shorter uniform, heavier eye makeup, and the humor that entertained them most days, I was never chosen.

My first kiss occurred that year with a stranger I met at a school social. He wasn't someone I liked. The kiss wasn't good. He smoked, and his breath stank of cigarettes. But I wanted to experiment like everyone else. He asked me to meet him on the overpass at the local train station the next day at four o'clock. I thought it might lead somewhere. *Could this be my first boyfriend?* I went there early to make sure I was there right at four.

I looked in every part of the station and left forty-five minutes later feeling like the stupidest girl alive, hoping he and his friends weren't hiding somewhere to laugh at me.

Later in high school, all my friends had infatuations with classmates. My attention, on the other hand, turned to the good-looking teachers. My fifteen-year-old friends couldn't quite understand why my gaze swung to the front of the classroom and not to the seat next to me. I was attracted to older men. I was attracted to older friends, too. Some people started calling me an old soul in my twenties, but in high school I didn't understand why I kept having premonitions of dating someone older than me. I didn't have any unhealed daddy issues; I have just always felt I was in a body fifteen years younger than my real age.

As I became wiser, I saw the crushes on unavailable teachers as an ingenious way to not risk rejection, which I had felt plenty of times. When I moved from my Catholic high school and my numbering-boys system to Templestowe High School, I heard along the gossip grapevine that Mr. Mansfield, the hunky physical education teacher, had to leave the school because of an intimate relationship with one of the older students. Whether it was true or not, I don't know, but it was enough to give me hope.

Mr. Quinn, my physics teacher, got more of my attention than the other teachers. He was short, muscular, and looked just bad boy enough. He always had his hair cut to the second closest shave possible, he had short facial hair, and he wore tracksuit pants that showed off how big his package was. This embarrassed me more than anything, as I was more interested in his biceps and his handsome smile. The day he invited me into his office was one of the most exciting days of the year. I walked into the narrow room that was sectioned off at the back of his classroom. My heart beat fast as his dimples came into form with a half-smile and he pulled out the chair for me. I sat down and showed him where I was stuck in my work. He was the only reason I was attempting physics. My brain didn't work in the way a physics student needed to think. He tried to explain how to predict linear motion, but I couldn't stop staring at the hair on his arm that lay on the desk beside me. I hadn't been this close to such a manly man I had a crush on before, especially one who was trying to help me. His arm hair looked so masculine. His body odor from his daily lunchtime run was strong enough to get my attention and subtle enough to not turn me off. It was a perfume I could get used to.

"Thanks, Mr. Quinn," I said as I left the tutorial, knowing that he thought nothing more of me than a pimply, rosy-cheeked, semi-goth-looking teenager who needed serious help with her physics. I was not the type of girl who could attract his attention. Gorgeous teachers were not willing to ruin their careers over me.

In my final year of high school, I felt lonelier by the day and desperate to escape. I had still not been asked out on a proper date by anyone. I kept asking what was wrong with me on the bus ride home each afternoon. During many of my lunch breaks I would head to the back corner of the school yard, where no one would see me, and sit under a tree and read spiritual texts, poems, and books. Most of my school friends rejected me, thinking I was too "up myself." They thought my interest in spiritual inquiry instead of getting drunk every weekend was my way of showing them that I felt superior. I felt so lonely when I was with people my own age and more connected to myself when I had my head in a book.

In my early twenties I believed I was going to die without ever having a boyfriend, though not from lack of trying. Not from a lack of nightclubs I frequented. What made the biggest difference in terms of getting attention was dyeing my hair platinum blonde. Burgundy hadn't worked, black with a blue stripe in the front hadn't worked, and my imitation of Nicole Kidman after perming my dead straight hair didn't work either. "Blondes have more fun" is not a myth. The first night I walked into a nightclub with blonde hair I felt I was like a flame, and the moths started fluttering. I was always one of the tallest girls, but now I was a tall beacon of light. The only problem was that the nightclub lights would make my blonde look even brighter, but once daylight hit, I looked atrocious. The cheap packaged hair dye I used was more yellow than blonde and it did not suit my porcelain white skin and rosy cheeks—at all.

My love life got worse during the first year of university. I had a huge crush on one of my best friends, Troy. He was funny, cute, and a great talker. We loved to talk for hours in the car after our Sunday night pizza outings and after our weekly youth group meetings. The crush lasted a year—until my best friend Fiona joined the group. One night as I was about to leave the pizza restaurant, Fiona leaned over and asked, "Can I speak to you outside before you go home?"

She looked like she had bad news.

"Sure," I said as I pushed my chair out and followed her outside. "What's up?" I asked in a supportive tone.

She looked at me with her naturally furrowed brow that was even more indented than usual and said, "Troy has just asked me to be his girlfriend."

Did I mention that most guys I knew considered Fiona drop-dead gorgeous?

My silence hung in the chilly air, and Fiona also remained quiet. I was mortified more than sad, as everyone knew I liked him. Now he wanted my best friend.

"I really like him too," she revealed. "We've been getting to know each other, and I didn't want to say anything because I know how much you like him."

Those words were like fingernails running down a chalkboard.

"Tell me you like him, Fi, and tell me he likes you, but do not utter the words 'I'm so sorry; I know you really like him,'" I said as I tried to breathe properly. I knew I would get over my crush. I just didn't know how I'd get over the humiliation.

I came to dread extended family gatherings. My younger sister Bridget had a boyfriend, my younger cousin had a fiancé, and I, the eldest of the family kids, had never brought anyone to meet the family. I dreaded the question I knew would come at least five times from different people: "Do you have a boyfriend yet?" After years of always having to say no, I would get angry. I dreamed of finally shocking my Nana or a country-bumpkin uncle by saying, "No, but I have a girlfriend I've just started dating and she's really hot!" I never had the guts.

I started to dread dinner parties with friends, too. Hanging out with the same friends I'd had for years and always being the only un-partnered one was like rubbing my face in my failure. If my love drought had only lasted for a few years, I might have handled it differently. I'd been single for ten years, and everyone was trying to figure out what my problem was. Perhaps the worst of it was that they were vocal about it. My only saving grace became my explanation that "I know he's not an Aussie. He's an American, which is why I feel such a pull to go there. I don't fit with Aussie males somehow."
The only ones who never once asked me what was wrong or worried about my loneliness were my parents. They were smart and sensitive enough to let me be.

Since I was never the one chosen, I developed my masculine side. I didn't want to need a man. I didn't want to rely on a man. I decided that women who wanted romantic love in their life were shallow and weak. I even put a bumper sticker on my first car—a 1975 red Toyota Celica—that proudly said *SINGLE and LOVING IT!* At the time I pretended to be proud of that sticker in the rear window, but internally I could feel the rejection and sadness that surrounded it. If I could have lined up all the women I knew who desperately wanted to be in a relationship, I would have been the first one in line. I went to watch *Dirty Dancing* in the cinema five times, for God's sake. I wanted love, but I was so embarrassed of never being chosen that I pushed that desire aside so no one else would know about it.

Given this background, it's easy to see what made meeting Robert so sweet. I showed all of my friends and family a photo of him, which I brought back home as proof and validation. I *could* attract a beautiful and masculine man.

CHAPTER 8

REVELATION OVER HOT COALS

After getting into the groove and completing Tony Robbins' Personal Power 2 cassettes once a year, I put going to one of his live events on my wish list. Six months before meeting Robert on that visit to the U.S., I attended Tony's Unleash the Power Within event. Fiona, still my best friend (with her third boyfriend by then, but who's counting) had an inexpensive ticket to share because her boss had bought them in bulk. I grabbed it.

We arrived together at the registration area on the first day, where we were handed our name badges and a form to sign from an overly cheery guy who used the word "awesome" in every sentence.

The release form I had to sign stated that I would take full responsibility for myself and would not hold the Tony Robbins company responsible if I hurt myself. Pretty standard, I thought. Then I read on as it shared in great detail the risks of fire walking. Fire walking is the ritual of walking over hot coals in your bare feet in order to stare fear in the face and do it anyway. It didn't only share all the risks of injury, but clearly stated, "You will be invited to walk over a 15–foot bed of hot coals in your bare feet. Sign this form to state that you are doing this of your own free will. You understand that your fire walk may lead to serious injury and possible death."

Death! What the hell?

I signed the form with my heart now in my stomach and walked into the huge indoor sports stadium along with five thousand others to the sound of loud music and the sight of a group of people in blue T-shirts dancing and jumping up and down on the stage to get the crowd going. Even though I enjoyed making fun of the overenthusiastic ushers, this was right up my alley. I had an ambitious streak, but it had been ignored because of fear. Fear of rejection, fear of getting hurt, fear that others would think I was arrogant. I was afraid that if I really put myself out there, I would eventually find out that I was not that extraordinary after all. I was more in love with my fantasy of becoming a star than working to make it a reality.

I loved personal development and practical psychology, and now I was with the best of the best. Tony came out to greet the crowd and took us on an adrenaline-filled ride that morning, with lots of fists punching the air and learning practical things I could implement immediately. All was going great until he dropped the bomb that we would be walking on hot coals in a few hours. I thought at least it would take a few days to prepare us for something so dangerous.

"I am purposely making you walk over coals on Day One so I can prove to you that it doesn't have to take a lot of time to get over your fears and do what you want to do," he bellowed from the stage.

I had never felt such terror anticipating an act I had to take. Tony showed us how to master our fear, which calmed the stadium somewhat, but then just as I was feeling ready to go he would say, "Now, you've got to be really careful when you walk, because you don't want to trip and fall directly on the coals, especially on your face. You don't want to burn the whole side of your face off."

"What the hell?" I shouted. No one could hear me, as everyone else was making their own terrified sounds.

He would start us with a chant so we would be ready to walk over those coals no matter how much fear we felt, and when we reached our highest point of confidence (if you could call it that), shock us with a story of people seriously injuring themselves.

It was time. Loud tribal drumming pounded in my ears. The crowd chanted "COOL MOSS, COOL MOSS," as Tony had taught us. Somehow this was to lull us into thinking that we weren't really walking on hot coals but on a bed of cool, sweet moss. We were like packed sardines trying to escape the stadium all at the same time. It took at least 45 minutes to chant and march all the way outside and get close enough to see the glow of the fire lanes. The crowd parted before me and there it was, a 15-foot lane of scorching-hot coals. I took my shoes off and bent down to place them in the row of shoes next to the lane. As I lifted myself, I was eye to eye with the coals. They were real. This was not a game. In a few seconds nothing would separate those coals from the soft, tender bottoms of my feet. Questions sparked by terror spun inside my head. *Would my naked, vulnerable feet soon be burned beyond recognition? Would I nose-dive and scar my face forever? Could I find a way to sneak into the line of those already finished without anyone noticing?*

All too soon, I was next. Suddenly, the lane master firmly grabbed my shoulder, pointed upward fiercely to make sure I didn't look down, and at the top of his lungs yelled, "GO!" I braced myself, looked up, and stepped onto the coals. *"One – two – three – four – cool moss – cool moss – cool moss – cool moss – nine – ten – eleven – twelve – COOL MOSS – COOL MOSS – COOL MOSS – COOL MOSS..."*

I did it. I had walked over hot coals and was unharmed. I felt like throwing up from the rush of adrenaline, so I bent over and put my head between my knees and stared at the asphalt and the other bare feet shuffling by. The main thing was that I didn't burn myself. I didn't get hurt. As the color started flooding my face again, I could celebrate that I was okay.

Six months later, right before my trip to the U.S., I served on the volunteer staff for the Unleash the Power Within event. I felt so passionate about how my life had changed in less than a year that I gave up a weekend to help make it an unforgettable experience for others. I didn't realize that meant I would be invited to face those coals again. This time I felt less frantic fear, but the concern that I would burn myself hadn't gone away. During staff training, which included learning how to help people across the coals, I kept hearing stories of people who burned themselves. A young, overweight woman said she was back for the eighth time, determined to walk the coals unharmed, as the first seven times she had burned her feet. I didn't want to walk the coals again. I was still scared, but I didn't want to be seen as afraid by the volunteers around me or by the eight friends I had brought with me to experience it this time.

After all the participants had taken their turn, my lane master asked, "Do you want to have your turn?" I said yes in a firm tone, but inside I was screaming *No!* I was again so scared of getting hurt. I didn't want to get hurt. I made myself push through it. I thought of cool moss, pumped myself with the routine I had relearned that day, and took that first step. *"One – two – three – four – cool moss – cool moss – OUCH! Not cool moss! Hot coals!"* It only took four steps for my brain to receive the emergency signal from my feet. *Get the hell out of there!* I kept going, and as I hit the grass at the end of the fire lane, I knew I had done damage. I quickly got hosed down and said as quietly as I could but loud enough to be heard, "I'm hurt; I burned myself." They took a look at the bottoms of my feet and sent me straight to first aid. There I was greeted with a cold bucket of water and a caring coach to help me through the process.

Sitting there sorry for myself, I tried to wrap my head around what had just happened. *What did I do wrong?* I looked around and noticed I was not the only one who was hurt that night. First aid was a meeting room full of people with their feet in buckets of water. Some were laughing and some were dejected.

The woman coach assigned to my burnt feet and ego kneeled in front of me and shared the words that would change the way I looked at my confusion about my love life forever.

"Whenever someone gets a 'hot spot' from their fire walk, it's a gift. Be quiet for a moment and ask your higher self—what is the message for you in this experience?"

She walked away to give me time to ask myself that question. In the silence, I heard that clear internal voice gently speak its wisdom: "The first time you did a fire walk, you moved through your fear and had the experience of not getting hurt and being okay. This time the experience is a greater gift for you. You moved through your fear, you got hurt, and you're still okay. You can open yourself and you may get hurt, but you'll be okay."

Over the next few weeks, many people tried to explain why I burned my feet. I wasn't present enough. I wasn't scared enough. I was too scared. I didn't walk fast enough. I didn't walk slow enough.

This woman reminded me to find my own reason. I remember her looking me in the eye and saying, "No one else can tell you why this happened. You have to ask your higher power—or whatever you call that—and discover the reason yourself."

My reason was clear: I got hurt and I was still okay.

As I sat with the coolness of the water soothing my feet, I realized I approached men I was attracted to in a way that I wouldn't get hurt. Everything I did was to maintain some self-protection. Protection from rejection, so it wouldn't be too obvious that I was interested in someone I fancied. Protection from being used, so I wouldn't show my feminine side much. Protection from being heartbroken, so I developed the habit of only flirting with married or partnered guys. That was safe—a way to not get hurt.

As I felt more confident with who I was and came out of my awkward, pimply phase, my friends would often comment, "I don't get it. You're attractive, funny, smart, and have a great personality. I don't get why men aren't asking you out." I didn't get it either at the time. It's only looking back that it became clear that my energy was sending the signal: "Don't break my heart. I don't want to get hurt."

CHAPTER 9

THE IMPATIENT WAIT

The four months away from Ashland were some of the hardest of my life. Not just because I was away from Robert, but I wasn't sure that the work visa would come through. I had to face the possibility of coming so close to love and having it snatched away from me. My poor mum received the brunt of my anxiety, which manifested as an arrogant, disgruntled, and immature daughter because I desperately wanted to get out of the family house and back to America. My parents had agreed that I could move back in with them to save some money before I made the permanent move to Ashland. It was hard enough for her to know that she was losing her eldest daughter to a country on the other side of the world, but for all her kindness, I was a bitch about it.

Depression started beckoning me. So much rode on my return, and yet I still hadn't received visa approval. I used the days to do as much vocal teaching as I could while offloading as many of my belongings as possible. I sensed I might not ever be coming back to Australia to live, so I sold practically everything. My music equipment, instruments, music CD collection, and furniture. My younger sisters received a new wardrobe. This somewhat lessened the sad state of affairs in my bank account, becoming my way of ceremoniously burning my bridges. I used the nights to study as much of the *Conversations with God* material as I could. I was honored to work with the famous Neale Donald Walsch and wanted to show my best when I arrived.

The best aspect of staying with Mum and Dad for four months was being with family. My parents had met playing tennis at the local tennis club in their small country town. They were both gifted athletically, and Dad was exceptional. Tall, slender, with dark chocolate hair, he was good at almost any sport he tried and had become one of the greatest Aussie Rules professional footballers of his time. Enough fans followed his career that a picture of me as his firstborn child made the local paper. Soon after my entrance into the world, a serious back injury cut his career short, though I never once heard a word of bitterness about it. All four of us kids called him MacGyver, because he was creative, handy, smart, and ingenious. He would never call himself gifted, but the proof was in everything he touched.

When we were young, he built many extensions onto our house. He designed and built elaborate playgrounds for the backyard, along with a deck for our pool. In our teens he made whatever our hobbies needed. He built a tennis court in the backyard when he found that most of us enjoyed playing. He converted the spare bedroom into a dance studio with walls of mirrors and a balance bar and turned it back when we outgrew it.

Even though his fuse was short after a frustrating day at work, the fire only lasted a few seconds. The only time I recall Dad being angry at me was when I was eight. I can't even remember what I did, but I do remember my punishment and it was delivered in the back seat of the car. He knew exactly what would get to me so I would never repeat what I had done. No, it was not a spanking. It was much worse. He opened the back door of the car and ordered, "You are not allowed to watch *Young Talent Time* this week. Go to your room, now!"

Young Talent Time was a variety show featuring young singers and dancers, and it was my favorite TV show. I'd sing and dance along with the musical numbers each week, and I dreamed that one day I would be on *Young Talent Time* too.

"No, Daddy. I promise I'll be good," I said as though pleading for my life. "I'll do whatever you want me to. Please let me watch *Young Talent Time*."

The punishment was set, though, and Dad wouldn't budge. I howled all the way to my room. It was the saddest week of my childhood.

What I loved most about Dad was how he was with my mother. Mum was his queen. He was tender with her. I never once heard him raise his voice to her. I don't recall him ever being frustrated with her. He would take her fair-skinned hand when he'd stand next to her. He'd come up behind her in the kitchen and put his arms around her slim waist and gently tickle her. Countless times he'd surprise her from behind and her reaction was always the same. She'd giggle shyly and say, "Stop it, Greg; stop it." Even as a 10-year-old I could tell she didn't mean it. Their affection and commitment to each other—and to us—was a given in my life. At the time I didn't realize how uncommon this respectful romance was.

Dad wasn't the only one who treated Mum like a queen. Everyone did. She taught in public primary schools her whole career. She always knew the right thing to do. She was the primary confidante for everyone. Her colleagues at school consulted her first if they sought advice. Her friends went to her before anyone else. Many of the women in our extended family visited her first, too. My mind was never far from whether I was living up to her high expectations. No one wanted to disappoint our mum. Her moral standards were as high as her perfect cheekbones and thin, perky eyebrows. Her integrity and modesty were broadcast through the elegant but understated clothing she wore and her perfect diction. My mum was beautiful. When I reached my thirties, I heard more often that I looked like her. I couldn't understand it, since Dad and I were the only brunettes in the family, but I was proud of the compliment.

When I finally got word that my visa application had been approved, my mood lightened in an instant. Even though they were sad at my leaving, my parents were happy for me. Mum had commented on how handsome Robert was. I know she was happiest for me because I had finally met a man who made me happy. Now all I needed to do was wait for the official immigration visa paperwork to be sent to the house, which was determined to be by May 2nd at the latest. I bought a ticket for an airplane departing May 7th, as my impatience to get back to Robert was growing by the minute.

For some unknown reason, it did not come in the mail by May 2nd, or May 3rd, or May 4th. After a nervous phone call to the U.S. immigration agency in Australia, they said it was approved. Still, it ended up on my doorstep one week later than they said it would. No one could give me a clear answer to why it was delayed. At the last minute I had to change my flight to one week later, which seemed like an eternity away from those gorgeous blue eyes.

REUNION

We hadn't talked or emailed much during the time I was away. Robert wasn't keen to talk much on the phone and I didn't want to push the issue. I wanted to keep him in pursuit and not instigate too much. I knew that much—to let guys make the moves. When his occasional email hit my inbox, I would read it at least ten times to squeeze every bit of meaning out of every single word.

I returned to Ashland on May 15th, 2002 via a Greyhound bus from San Francisco—seven days later than originally planned. As the familiar mountain ranges came into view, memories started to flood back. What would our first meeting back together be like? Our last email exchange had been eight days earlier, and we'd agreed to be open to whatever happened when I arrived. I anticipated our soul connection leading to many years of love and adventure.

Julia was the volunteer that the Conversations with God Foundation chose to pick me up from the bus station. We had many eager questions for each other, as we were going to be roommates now. I felt I made a friend right away. She'd been working for the Foundation for just a few weeks. I told her of my desire to learn from Neale's teachings and the short version of the story about Robert. She was a romantic too, so she couldn't wait to hear the juicy details of our reunion.

After arriving at the shared housing, I met the other volunteers and unpacked some essentials. I called Robert that night to let him know that I was safe, but he didn't answer, so I left a voicemail. He called back the next day, but it was my turn to miss his call. I dialed into the voice-messaging service after one of my housemates told me there was a message waiting.

Ah...that accent! I sighed as I started to listen to his voice.

"Hi there, Rach; I'm glad you got here safe and well. I got your message. I'm going away for the weekend, so I'm wondering if we could see each other on Monday when I get back. I might be out of cell range quite a bit, so I'll plan on dinner on Monday night. If that doesn't work, leave a message for me here. Have a great weekend."

I hung up and stared at the phone in confusion. Monday?

I called him back immediately. No answer. Just voicemail. I summoned the sexiest, warmest, and most assured voice that I could muster under the circumstances and left a quick message saying I was looking forward to seeing him on Monday night.

As the weekend hours went by, I ran out of things to do to keep myself busy. I'd already unpacked my one suitcase and guitar case. I had nothing to decorate my new bedroom with. I walked around the tiny town, feeling nauseous. *Why did he go away without me? Why was he not here to greet me after I flew halfway around the world?* My mind started playing out all sorts of scenarios until Monday night finally came.

His Volkswagen hatchback pulled up in front of the house. I saw him through the glass panel beside the front door and my heart pounded so hard, I was scared to hug him lest he feel my nerves. I opened the door and walked down the short garden path to meet him at his car. As my eyes fixed on his handsome figure, I felt like I was watching a slow-motion moment in an action movie. He swung out and around the car, gave me that unforgettable smile, a friendly hug, polite kiss on the cheek, and opened the car door for me.

"How are you?" he asked softly, without giving much away about how he was feeling.

"I'm doing really well," I lied.

"I remembered you love Thai food, and there's a great place around the corner."

He started the engine and pulled away from the curb.

The conversation felt a little stilted and forced. His car was small, and I didn't feel confident enough to turn and look at him. I focused inanely on the black knobs and dials on the dashboard. I reminded myself that my case of nerves was normal, given that we were out of the rhythm of seeing each other each day. The relationship got off to an intense start and we'd been apart for four months.

As he opened the door to the restaurant for me, I was reminded of what a gentleman he was. We were greeted by a fish tank and a middle-aged Asian woman who wasn't even as tall as my shoulder. The paper decorations and kitschy decor surprised me. The place was almost empty. We sat down in one of the booths near the window, and with a grin the size of China, the woman asked what we would like to drink.

"I'll just have some water, no ice," Robert stated.

"I'll have the same." Even though I had presumed a glass of wine would be in order.

He asked me about my first few days of settling in to the new surroundings and about who else was living at the volunteer house.

I lied again, telling him I had a fun weekend with new friends. I enjoyed re-acquainting myself with the lines on his face while we talked.

I didn't know what question to ask him other than the one that had stressed me all weekend.

I finally asked, "How was your weekend? Where did you go?"

"It was good. I went to the coast to one of my favorite spots." He fell silent after that announcement, waiting for my reaction. I was hopelessly confused. I felt he had something to say but didn't want to say it.

And then he did.

"I met someone else," he said apologetically.

Stunned silence. My mind went blank. He didn't break the silence.

"When?"

"I met her seven days ago." He kept his voice steady and unemotional.

"How?"

"We started talking outside the co-op and then realized we were walking in the same direction and had a strong connection on our walk home."

"What's her name?" I said, trying to sound like I was not going to break down in front of him.

He didn't want to say, but he did. "Her name is Rachael."

More silence.

"Given the serendipitous timing of all of this, I thought it might be a sign and I had to pursue it with her. I'm sorry."

That was the moment when my heartbreak exploded. He thought it was a sign! *A fucking sign? Fucking serendipity?*

They had gone away together for the weekend, and he sheepishly told me they were falling in love. He shared how strong the connection was and that he couldn't let go of it for now. I couldn't believe what I was hearing. I tried so hard to look like I was okay about this. I tried to look like I was enjoying my green curry. My smile was that deeply saddened fake smile I saw on Hilary Clinton's face at Donald Trump's inauguration. There was no hiding it. I was not happy for him.

How could you four months earlier have fallen so madly in love with a person you said you felt you had a soul contract with, and now you are doing it again? My forced smile didn't stick for long. The fortune cookies came and I stuffed mine into my handbag, not caring if it smashed into little pieces.

"I'm ready to go. I have a big first day at work tomorrow," I said with a touch of disdain.

He drove me back home. I got out of the car without touching him. I walked in the door of the volunteer house, straight up to the stairs to my new bedroom, where my guitar lay next to my one empty suitcase, with nothing hanging on the walls, and let myself fall into a very ugly cry. Julia comforted me later that night with hot tea and chocolate chip cookies. All the while the realization sank in—I had just given up my life, sold everything, and moved to the other side of the world for a guy who was not interested in me after all.

Grief had its way with me. For weeks I tried to keep my mind off Robert by getting acquainted with everyone at the CWG Foundation. Everyone was very nice, but I was heartbroken. I was mortified at the prospect of telling my family and friends back home who had heard so much about this dream man. *This cannot be happening,* I pleaded with God. Many nights I wanted to scream. Some nights my pillow bore the brunt of my devastation so everyone in the rest of the house wouldn't hear me. I wanted to find out who this other Rachael was. *This has got to be one very bad cosmic joke,* I thought. I was supposed to be back in Ashland seven days earlier. I was supposed to be the one talking to him outside the co-op. I was supposed to be the Rachael who was looking into those blue eyes and eating brown rice, tofu, and kale. But I was not the one chosen. I didn't know I could cry so hard for so long.

They say all clouds have silver linings. I believe that. Sometimes grief dulls us, and sometimes grief sharpens us and makes us more aware. My silver lining from the cloud of Robert was Rumi.

I fell in love with Rumi because of Bill Kauth. Bill is one of the founding fathers of New Warrior Training, which to date has led over 50,000 men through it worldwide and has received huge acclaim. The CWG Foundation had the entire staff attend the Warrior-Monk Training, which was also created by Bill's brilliance. When I first heard Rumi's poems float from Bill's lips, I was blissful. My favorite of his poems is "Love Dogs." The passion, the polarity, and the peace he wrote about hit my heart and launched a desire to give my life to be one of those Love Dogs. I was still hurting from Robert's betrayal, but I was healing in more ways than I knew.

This thirteenth-century Persian poet, theologian, and Sufi mystic spoke of an enlightened experience that satisfied every one of my senses. Rumi offered relief from the pain that cut deep from losing in love and presented hope that someday I would have what I most longed for. Rumi not only soothed my heartbreak and disappointment but opened the possibility that my desire for deep love was my answer. My grief and my willingness to cry out for what I wanted was my gift.

LOVE DOGS

One night a man was crying,
Allah! Allah!
His lips grew sweet with the praising, until a cynic said,
"So! I have heard you calling out,
but have you ever gotten any response?"
The man had no answer to that.
He quit praying and fell into a confused sleep.

He dreamed he saw Khidr, the guide of souls,
in a thick, green foliage.
"Why did you stop praising?"
"Because I've never heard anything back."
"This longing you express is the return message."
The grief you cry out from draws you toward union.
Your pure sadness that wants help is the secret cup.
Listen to the moan of a dog for its master.
that whining is the connection.
There are love-dogs no one knows the names of
Give your life to be one of them.

As the most painful rejection of my life coursed through my system, I hoped the work at the CWG Foundation would provide a desperately needed distraction. It was a distraction, for sure, but not the one I expected.

• C H A P T E R   1 1 •

THE MAN IS NOT THE MESSAGE

I was finally going to meet my favorite author of all time. Neale Donald Walsch had written the *Conversations with God* series, which had a profound effect on my life. I'd first picked up Book One on the side table of Satina's guest bedroom and had since devoured all five books he'd written up until then. I listened to Neale's voice on CD almost every night in my tiny Australian bedroom back home. As I stared up at the soft glow of the planetary stickers on the ceiling I had put there in my teens, I had a clear sense that the CWG work would be instrumental in my life. Neale was an actor as well as an author, and an entertaining, uplifting, and stirring quality came through his deep voice. I received insight after insight as a young woman who was starting to awaken to more complex spiritual concepts.

I'd seen Neale from a distance five months earlier at the winter retreat I'd attended with Satina. We'd made the trip from

Australia just for it. He ignited emotion, vulnerability, and awareness like a master craftsman. This was his art. Mesmerizing an audience was effortless for him. He was a man of polar opposites, which made him even more intriguing. He could cuss and tell dirty jokes like a dark-edged comedian, dressed in what looked like a cross between a pair of white pajamas and a Kundalini yoga outfit, wearing a large medallion around his neck. He radiated power and authority as he sat in a big rose-red fabric armchair on the raised stage, and he revealed the most tender of underbellies as he hugged people in severe emotional pain. His spiritual message reached my head, heart, and gut. I was eager to be his student. I had no idea of what was to unfold, however.

Our first meeting occurred in June 2002 at the height of his fame in the spiritual author world. I was psyched and a little nervous at the same time. Everyone who had worked at the Conversations with God Foundation for a while seemed very loyal and thought a lot of Neale, but I was confused by one thing that I'd been told several times in my first few weeks of working there. It was the statement, "The man is not the message."

Neale had called an emergency staff meeting the night before, so all twelve on staff were ready in the front lobby, most nervous, when the tall gray-haired, bearded, blue-eyed, somewhat overweight Neale blew into the room like a gale force wind. I couldn't help thinking he looked like Santa Claus. I later found out he had a preoccupation with Santa Claus, which included a ritual at Christmas when he would set out over 300

Santa Claus statues that he owned in various positions inside his mansion, nestled in the hills just outside of Ashland.

He didn't greet anyone. He sat down and kept his gaze fixed to the beige carpet as he cleaned his wire-framed glasses with the edge of his shirt. At first I couldn't figure out if the creases between his eyes meant he was angry or contemplative. The last of us found a seat in the circle. Since I was the new kid, I waited for the more senior staff members to take a seat first. Big mistake. That strategy forced me to take the only remaining chair left, which was right next to my new guru, who had opted not for his spiritual garb but blue jeans, white T-shirt, and a brown leather jacket. I've always been a pretty good reader of people's energy, so as I sat down I knew this was not the time to introduce myself as the new gal who'd come all the way from Australia to volunteer for nine months.

Since I sat next to him in the circle formation, I couldn't see his face and didn't have the courage to turn my head. But as that familiar voice started to speak, I had a prime viewing position to see the reactions of everyone else on staff to their chosen leader.

"I can't believe this has happened—again!" Those words came out with extreme irritation, which made me sit a little straighter in my chair. He continued to unleash his frustration as his voice got louder. He reached a crescendo five minutes into his high-volume rant and maintained it for the next 30 minutes as his yelling reverberated off my body like loud, offensive music pounding from a speaker. He shamed and demeaned the staff as a whole while singling out particular members with a more lavish dose.

Neale had wanted the staff to reach a goal, but they hadn't, for reasons unclear to me. The sonic ripples of blame were so forceful that it put me in a state of shock. I felt like I was watching a movie where I couldn't quite understand the story line. A few brave souls spoke up and defended other team members, which Neale didn't mind. He honored pushback. He liked a debate—the more spirited, the better. At the end of his tirade I looked around at the group, and they looked like a weary team that had been defeated in a game they knew from the start they couldn't win.

Then Neale turned to me and said in a soft, soothing voice, "Are you okay? You don't look well."

Caught off guard, I said, "I'm fine," in an unconvincing tone.

That was my introduction to the man who spoke with God. I wasn't shattered. I was confused. I felt like all my energy had been sucked out of me. The staff looked like they had just had all the life sucked out of them. Looking back, I was given one of the best lessons of my life that day. The man is not always the message.

After he left the office and climbed into his black luxury car, senior team members Joanna and Patty came over to check on me. I learned later they were accustomed to cleaning up this sort of mess.

"You look pale; are you okay?"

"Yes, you look like you've seen a ghost."

"I'm fine. It's just my pale skin." I kept my words to a minimum. I didn't yet know what was politically correct to say about the tirade I had just witnessed.

Joanna took me by the hand and led me over to the mail desk, only yards away. A simple lavender sign with the word *Peace* hung over the cork message board with instructions for the volunteers who opened the mail. She sifted through a pile of opened handwritten mail and chose three for me.

"Read these today. Especially this one." She was pointing to a letter from the San Quentin Penitentiary with a prisoner number under the return address. "His work has changed hundreds of thousands of lives. I love Neale. He's been one of my greatest mentors, and at the same time he can be difficult. Have no doubt, my dear, he is a master—but every master has a shadow."

Her eyes glistened and her heart was sincere. I wanted to fall right into her triple-D-size bosom and let my shock turn into tears. Instead I smiled politely and kept my mouth shut.

During another check-in that day with Patty, I realized that Neale's outbursts were a common occurrence. The veteran members of his foundation were used to it. As months went by and I deepened my friendship with staff members, many admitted that they had father issues, boundary issues, or experiences of abuse in some form when they were growing up. Somehow this was playing out for them again. I came from an almost perfect parental situation growing up and had never experienced anything like it, which added to my confusion about what had just happened. I had a massive headache for three days.

A week later, the staff had their monthly summer afternoon play day. The activity that month was softball.

Julia was quickly becoming my closest friend on staff, so we drove together over to the field in her car. In her early fifties and also single, she had been just as enamored with Neale and the Conversations with God message when she decided to give up six months of her life to volunteer.

It was a perfect Oregon day. The sun beamed directly above, and we were surrounded in all directions by mountains and wooded homes nestled into the ridges wherever they could find a space in that gorgeous valley. It was easy to understand why this was an upscale getaway for stressed-out Californians. Being a city girl all my life, I wasn't used to such big skies and pine forests. I was still acclimatizing to the deer on the sidewalks and the lack of traffic while my new friends were adjusting to my accent. In those days I could be hard to understand. It was thick, with Aussie slang mixed in liberally.

Other minor celebrities in town joined us for the friendly competition because they heard Neale would be there. Author and singer/songwriter Jimmy Twyman arrived and hugged everyone as if they were his best friends. Jeff, a local morning radio host, drew my attention with his mysterious handsomeness as he took the pitcher's mound. I guessed he was 22 years my senior and that every woman there was imagining how that ball felt in his strong, manly hands.

Neale showed up late in jeans and a baseball cap. The energy changed in an instant as he walked onto the field. His intensity followed him everywhere he went. I went into observer mode, as I often do when I don't feel comfortable. I noticed who was competitive and who liked to just have fun. I was doing neither. Julia had torn something significant in her leg between first and second base in the first ten minutes of the game and had been carried off to hospital. That was enough to keep me on the sidelines.

The jostling humorous remarks between Jimmy and Neale were entertaining. Jimmy was rising through the ranks of the spiritual teacher world quickly because he was showing people how to bend spoons with their minds. That gave Neale plenty of material for sarcasm. Jimmy was down-to-earth, funny, and approachable. I was still trying to decipher whether Neale was safe enough to approach for a proper introduction.

I had imagined before leaving Australia that he would be a soft, patient, wise, easy-to-hug teddy bear. Instead, I again witnessed a man yelling at the top of his lungs at his staff, like a child who wasn't getting his way. It was supposed to be a game of light-hearted softball, but he found ways to twist himself into knots and scream at Ed, our half-bald, cute audiovisual guy who served as umpire. I went home with another massive headache.

Still, it was no accident that my first job in the USA was with one of the most talented authors, speakers, and facilitators I have ever seen. I now do almost exactly the same type of work.

There is no doubt in my mind that Neale is brilliant at his work. The way he could facilitate awareness in others was comparable to none other I'd seen up to that point. The way he could share a story that transported everyone to awe was something I wanted to learn. Neale was a gift to me. Just not a gift I consciously asked for. He was about to dish out some of the hardest lessons of my life.

CHAPTER 12

SPIRITUAL COLLEGE

I'd accomplished the miracle of moving to America, but I was beaten down. I was on the other side of the world with no friends, no family, and very few possessions. Now the two men for whom I had packed up my life (personally on one hand and professionally on the other) had fallen off their respective pedestals with dramatic thuds.

I vacillated between two questions: *Did I do something wrong that led my dream so far off track?* and *Was this my Higher Power stepping in to save me from a worse fate?* It was a conundrum for me, and I didn't have the answer to either.

To regain my faith, I buried myself in spiritual books and went to as many workshops as I could afford. Living in Ashland and working for the Conversations with God Foundation was my spiritual college. Ashland was a town of 20,000 people, mostly made up of New Age hippies, dedicated spiritual seekers, and California escapees. Prospects of becoming a country music star there were dismal at best. It seemed every spiritual guru lived there—Gary Zukav, Jean Houston, Gangaji, James Twyman, and Neale, to name a few. It was a mecca for those searching for enlightenment. Almost every weekend I dabbled in some new metaphysical, therapeutic, psycho-spiritual, or dance experience, nourishing the joyful core of me and setting aside the loneliness and sadness that had become my steadiest companions.

My first job at the CWG Foundation bored me. I had begun at the bottom of the food chain as a volunteer in their volunteer house, sharing with four other people. I performed very basic tasks for the first nine months. I answered phones, opened mail (many times in gloves and masks at the height of the 2002 anthrax scare), and helped out with customer service and data entry. I didn't mind doing menial tasks for a while. I thought of it like a holiday. There was no music business to run and no gigs or singing students to find and enroll. I had a monthly stipend of a few hundred dollars for food and a place to live.

I found I was good on the phone with people—as long as they could understand me. I answered the phone in my thick Aussie accent with "Hi, Conversations with God Foundation, how may I help you?" Many people would respond with complete silence for a few moments while I'm sure they asked themselves, *What did she just say?*

Sometimes I would hear them giggle for a few seconds at the sound of my voice. At times I wanted to say, "I'm speaking English, people! It's the same language!" but I held my Australian tongue. I was well aware that Americans loved Australians, thanks to Crocodile Dundee as well as the Sydney

Olympics. However, I hadn't realized how much they loved hearing the accent. It was extremely satisfying to stand out as unique in that way, though I had to learn to say a few key words in an American accent so the number of "Sorry, can you repeat that?" comments didn't drive me bananas.

After six months passed, my blue jeans told me I had eaten too many chocolate chip cookies and my heart, although shattered, knew I wanted to stay. I had much to learn that wasn't available anywhere else. There was a feminine empowerment workshop on practically every corner on every day of the week. Over time many of the staff at the Foundation became my second family, and they took care of me when I needed it. My friendships were deepening, my state of consciousness expanding, mentors were showing up, and I had the feeling I wanted to live in Ashland for many years to come.

The application to extend my internship visa for another nine months was pretty simple. I just had to declare that at the end of this next nine-month period that I would leave the country and use what I had learned to further my career in Australia. I filled out the forms, all the while thinking, "This gives me nine more months to pull another rabbit out of a hat."

After my visa extension was approved, I started to feel the call to do something more meaningful with the Foundation and help out more in the community. Cedric handed me the keys to his Chevy rust bucket after leaving the Foundation. That car gave me more independence and freedom. I bought a second-hand framed picture of Marilyn Monroe from a thrift store to hang on my bedroom wall along with a plant to signify I was there for the long haul.

I was almost ready to start looking for love again, but the thought lingered that I would never find something as good as what I'd found with Robert. He did call me once to check in on me and see how I was doing. My attempt at sounding like life was wonderful would not have won me an Academy award. I ran into him on Main Street a month later. Thankfully, he was not escorting the other Rachael. I tried to dodge him by slipping into a nearby crystal shop and pretending I had enough money to buy something. Unfortunately, he'd already seen me, so I was forced to have a stilted interaction with another fake smile. I couldn't get the vision of him looking so fit and happy out of my head for weeks. I knew where he worked out—I didn't go there. I knew his favorite bar—I didn't go anywhere near there. I knew his favorite restaurant, his favorite spot by the creek, and of course where he lived. I gave them all as wide a berth as possible.

When I had some peaceful moments of quiet, I would ask the question to the voice that had guided me before: "Where shall I go to meet my perfect partner?" The only message I received was "Go to Toastmasters." Attending a speaking club was not the sexy answer I was expecting, and it took me almost a year to take the message seriously and attend my first meeting. Even though I wasn't physically attracted to any of the men, I made some really good friends that restored some faith that there were conscious, smart, creative, masculine guys in town. Gary and Paul became good friends at my local club. They were great speakers, and we had a love for spirituality and music in common. Almost all the men at Toastmasters were partnered—which was part of the problem. Actually, the problem spanned the entire town. There was one single guy for every ten gorgeous, slim, sexy single women. Toastmasters and our social time afterward ended up being the highlight of my week. The fact that my favorite men were all examples of what I was looking for—creative, fun, committed to growth, and grounded—gave me hope.

Toastmasters was the place I conquered my extreme nervousness toward public speaking—to the point I started to feel that I might want to be a professional speaker one day. I could sing all day long onstage and feel supremely confident, but my biggest fear would be that the guitarist would break a string. I dreaded hearing the words, "Just talk to the crowd and keep them engaged while I change my string." That would mean at least two minutes I would have to fill. My mind would suddenly turn the crowd into people who judged me. I would hesitate, pull the microphone closer—and then go blank. The coolest thing to ever came out of my mouth in one of those moments was, "Hey. I hope you are having a good night." And then I'd fall silent for the other one minute and fifty-five seconds while blushing and trying to look like I had to fix my tambourine.

After the visa renewal I was ready to move my career forward. I had already drawn the conclusion that my soul's purpose was not to sing or become a songwriter. My days of performing at bars and functions where no one paid much attention had burned me out. I was done entertaining people merely for entertainment's sake. I felt my true calling was to help facilitate others in their spiritual growth and their ability to express themselves fully. I kept hearing a mantra from different places: "Just do what you love and the money will follow."

I thought that was the most brilliant saying I had ever heard—until I realized it wasn't true! I tried to find people who wanted to hire me as their life coach, but no one volunteered. I tried to run a small women's workshop—and only my housemates came. I knew the next chapter of my soul's work was to fall head over heels and commit to this newfound love of spirituality and personal growth. I just didn't know exactly how it was going to happen or how I was going to replenish my bank account each week. I was sick of living with one print on the bedroom wall and one plant. I was tired of wearing the too-small clothes that I had scrunched as tightly as I could into my one suitcase and the underwear I had stuffed in the body of my guitar for the trip here. I started to look around the CWG Foundation to see where I could help out more. It became clear that the area where I had the most desire to help was the area where they needed my help the most.

Patty had been anointed with the title Director of Education a few years prior, since she'd been with Neale since the early days, soon after he'd written *Conversations with God*, his first published book. The messages in the book came to him when his life was in shambles. He'd already had three marriages end in divorce, nine children, had been homeless for a stint, and by his own description had become an angry and desperate person.

When the book took off, a small group of friends rallied around him to keep up with the fan mail pouring in from readers. Neale liked giving all the main roles to those closest to him. He had an inner circle and an outer circle. Patty was in the inner circle.

The Foundation had been trying to design an education program for years, but it was unrealistic for anyone to expect Patty to fulfill it with all her other roles. She was the chief financial officer, the retreats coordinator, and one of Neale's main confidantes, and with her fast-paced family life she had no hope of devoting the necessary amount of time. The education program was meant to attract CWG enthusiasts and teach them how to teach CWG to others through CWG circles, workshops, or their own retreats. The Foundation had received hundreds of requests of this nature and knew if it was done well, it would likely become the highest revenue-producing program by far that they'd ever had. Plus, it would get the message out to the world exponentially—which was always the Foundation's highest intention. Neale's frustration grew each year the plan didn't come to fruition. His quarterly rant about it not being done made Patty feel like she'd just drank a concoction of shame and resentment. This made me want to help her even more.

I approached Patty and put forward my case. "I can help. I have time, even with my other roles. I can be your support person if you would like," I offered. "I could do some research and get a draft of something that we can work with."

"That would be fantastic," she said. "Once you've done some preliminary work, I can look at it and see how it meshes with Neale's ideas for the program."

I started to craft the draft of the curriculum, which took about three weeks. I had lots of fun in the creation phase. I asked myself the question, *What do people really need if they are going to master the art of speaking, training, and coaching using the Conversations with God material?* I knew it had to include speaker training, and given my membership at Toastmasters, I had contacts who could teach that part. I knew it had to include training from Neale to transfer his philosophy to the students so they would clearly understand the way Neale wanted the CWG material to be taught beyond him. I knew the students needed better coaching skills, and there was already a CWG Coaching Services organization run by my friend Paul Clark at Toastmasters and Jim Fritz. With all these ideas coalescing, the CWG Leadership Education Program was born—at least on a Word document on my computer.

I emailed the document to Patty, including the modules the students would need to complete and a list of suggested trainers who could teach the portions of it that Neale wouldn't along with the budget—and finally, the price. It was a year-long program, and my proposal was to set the cost at $10,000 for the year or they could do a FastTrack version over three months for $12,000.

Patty liked my proposal and presented it to Neale. He loved it, even though he was skeptical about whether Patty could follow through on the grand plan. He'd gotten his hopes up before, so his concern was justified. I was finally a blip on his radar. We'd still not even had a proper conversation, though. Many starry-eyed fans had come and gone quickly after realizing it wasn't the House of Nirvana they thought it would be. For that reason I'm sure he didn't have much faith that my visit from Australia would lead to much. A few tweaks were made in the budget I proposed, but essentially it was passed and I was off and running.

I got Patty's permission to write the copy for the website where we would announce the program, to design a logo for the program, and to start to negotiate contracts with contractors who would teach the parts that Neale wasn't interested in teaching. After all that I had to start enrolling people, as I was the only one on staff who really knew what the program entailed in enough detail. At the time I didn't stop to think how easy this was for me, even though I'd never done anything like it before.

Success was immediate. Within six months I had filled all available spots in the program through phone and in-person discussions with CWG fans. It brought in close to half a million dollars for the Foundation. Praise was delivered—mostly to Patty, but I didn't care. I loved the joy of creating the experience. I was able to bring the best transformational teachers together—whom now I would essentially be learning from as I sat in the back of the room, helping at all the different types of training.

I had to fly under the radar in order to protect some of the egos in the group who wanted to be the ones in charge. That was pretty easy. I just let them know who was boss. They were. Who was running the program? They were. Who were the most important people in the organization? They were. I initially kept my head down, working on the next year's expansion of the program, but my ego would get me in trouble soon enough.

CHAPTER 13

MY LITTLE GIRL

I've always had a push-pull dynamic between wanting and not wanting to be seen. I desire attention at times and want no attention on me other times. I believe this is a conundrum for most people, but I've had it to extremes.

In my current work with women spanning all ages, races, and orientations, I've come to realize that being truly seen by someone who is present and non-judgmental is like food and water for our soul. Attention is that important. Without it, our spirits starve. It's easy to tell who receives lots of healthy, loving attention. They are alive and happy, though it may not appear they need that attention. At the same time, though, when attention is focused on us, it can be terrifying. It can spin us into self-consciousness, trying too hard, or even feeling traumatized.

The part of me that has been most fearful of being seen is a younger part of myself, who I call "Miss Goody Two-shoes." She's five years old and has dead straight brown hair down to her shoulders with bangs, freckles, and rosy checks. She always sits in the front two rows, wants to please her teacher, and would like to see straight A's on her report card. She is shy and smart, and to get in trouble would be the worst humiliation.

Fast-forward thirty years. Can you imagine the terror she felt when I (my adult self) had the courage to own my desire for the first time that I wanted to speak onstage in front of hundreds of people and kick some ass? Can you imagine the tight grip she had on my solar plexus when I first had the confidence to say, *I am going to shake things up and tell the truth that some people will find hard to hear?* She freaked out! To this day she still clenches my jaw when I want to step out of my comfort zone and risk being and having more. She knows that will mean more responsibility, and she doesn't want that. She knows someone could get angry at me, which would be extremely frightening.

Everyone has a frightened little boy or girl inside them. The younger part of us never goes away. The empowering question is how to relate to that part so it doesn't run our lives or keep the brakes on when trying to move forward as a more expansive person. When we feel fear, it is rarely the person today that is scared; it's that younger part of us. If a new way to talk with this younger part is not found, we can keep the brakes on per-manently. Many times I couldn't figure out why something scared me and made me procrastinate on something I really wanted to achieve. When I realized it wasn't the current me but a younger part, the brakes released and forward motion accelerated.

I found an entertaining solution a few years ago when Miss Goody Two-shoes and I wanted different things. What I say to her now, just before I go onstage, is this: "Hi, sweetie; I know you are feeling scared. I want you to know that you don't have to deal with the people out there. I will. If they get nasty or judge me or start getting tough with me, I can handle it. I've been doing this for a long time. That is not your job, that is my job."

I feel her tension relax inside my body.

I now converse with my inner child as much as I can. I talk to her and reassure her. If your inner child feels loving attention, they feel safe and won't try to hold you back. I've learned not to resist the innocent one inside me. I wish I had known how to talk to my inner child before I met Neale. He triggered my little girl more than anyone. At the time I didn't recognize that Miss Goody Two-shoes was taking over every small interaction we had.

I wanted Neale's positive attention, just like everyone else, and I didn't want Neale's negative attention, just like everyone else. Neale had a habit of singling people out.

"Why can Julia do this and the rest of you can't? Y'all should spend time with her to figure out what she's doing that makes her so good at her job."

It made everyone, including Neale's hero of the day, feel like a soggy wet rag. I suspected Neale felt his job was to come off his hill, blast into the office, and stir up the energy, as that would somehow spur us to better performance.

The other reason he singled people out was their looks. Volunteers continually passed through. They became house-mates, and usually only the beautiful ones were invited to his house for long, private "get-to-know-you" conversations. The beautiful ones were invited to the same weekly gatherings at his home as his close friends. They were told to bring their swimsuits and soak in his hot tub under the stars. I was never invited and was glad for that. I don't believe I would have fit in.

As I worked at the Foundation over the ensuing months and years, I didn't know why I was never included in inner-circle gatherings. I had now run two successful Leadership Education Programs, which had made the nonprofit Foundation over a million dollars. I didn't want to get into a hot tub with Neale, but I was curious why I'd not had even a one-on-one conversation with him that felt halfway normal.

Whenever I'd get around Neale, I'd feel insecure. My little girl showed up. She didn't want to get into trouble, so she stayed silent. I would feel his awkwardness and averted my eyes. I could connect with his onstage personality, but I couldn't relate to his offstage personality at all.

Julia and Joanna at the Foundation were masters at interacting with Neale. They were both warm, feminine, charming, and giggled at his almost-funny jokes as well as the ones that hit the mark. They perceived—and in turn received—the teddy bear in Neale. Patty did not have as much precision in the finer points of winning Neale's positive attention, but they were as close to family as you could get. In one of our meetings, Patty caught a hint of judgment in my voice and with gentleness put me back in my place. "He's like family. You forgive your family for their downfalls. You don't judge them and they won't judge you. Family runs deep here."

When someone would intimidate me, which Neale often did, I would tend to get really serious. I couldn't smile at those times to save my life. It was as if I tried to lead with my intelligence, but it never came off that way. I'm sure I merely looked judgmental and stiff. I had befriended all his friends on staff. I did well at laughing at his jokes. I saw myself as more socially adept than most people around him.

So why couldn't I befriend Neale? In the entire time of working for him we'd never had a normal conversation like I had with everyone else. I mostly assumed that we were not much alike, that he didn't really like me much, and that he didn't know what to say to someone who was so serious. Since he was one of the most famous spiritual authors of our time who had sold over ten million books, he didn't need to be liked, especially not by me.

Eventually I had my turn as Neale's favorite to single out in team meetings. As we all sat in our usual circle formation, he motioned with his head toward me. "Look what she is doing. Why can't the rest of you meet with her to find out why she can do her job and you can't?" Now the group looked at me as the one who made them feel like a soggy wet rag. I didn't want to be singled out. I didn't want extra praise. It did not feel safe to excel. This was not the kind glowing report card that made my little girl feel comfortable. She was more scared of him than ever.

● CHAPTER 14 ●

THE CLEARING

By the second year of leading the Leadership Program at the Foundation, I wanted more autonomy. I've always been an independent spirit—not rebellious, just independent. I'd never worked for anyone else for more than a few months, which was back in my college days. I was an entrepreneur at heart, even though I wouldn't have called myself that back then. For the most part they let me run my own department at the Foundation, and that arrangement was perfect, as I'm not built to ask permission or to handle bureaucratic red tape. I liked to go from concept to creation at the speed of a Lamborghini. They saw me as a go-getter early on, which worked well for them.

I was finally given one of the few offices with a door. I felt a little claustrophobic within the tiny space with no windows, but a small skylight helped, and the arrangement was private. I loved the role I had created for myself. I was feeling happier by the day, feeling I was living my purpose. Part of why Neale and I worked well together in accomplishing his dream was that he stayed out of my way and I stayed out of his. Even if he didn't like me that much, he respected what I did for his movement. He was not a micromanager with me. He never once raised his voice or got angry at me—and I made a few huge mistakes that would have set him off on a tirade had it been someone else. His energy in any room was impactful. He was never invisible. He always had something to say—just not to me.

The most memorable words he personally delivered to me in the six years of working for him came in written form. I unwrapped his Christmas gift to me at the annual Christmas party and discovered a signed copy of his new manuscript printed on standard white paper, yet to be published. I flicked through the first few pages, and on the title page it read:

> *To my Miracle Worker. You have created*
> *something I have wanted for so long. Thank you*
> *so much for all that you are.*
> *Love Neale*

I felt some peace that he saw me that way. I had never served someone else in their mission before, so this lessened the negative self-judgment I had started to feel, given that I had let my dreams of music, spiritual life coaching, and standing in front of an audience fall away.

Given that gift and its message, I was confused and apprehensive when Rita, our third executive director in twelve months, called me into her office to say that Neale wanted her to mediate a discussion between us.

"He has some important matters to talk to you about and he wants me to mediate," she said. "That's all I can tell you right now. Let's schedule a time for Wednesday afternoon."

"Okay," I replied as the blood rushed out of my face. *Mediate?* I thought. That's a strong choice of words. I sorted through the file cabinet in my mind for what I might have done to irritate him. I came up blank.

Neale had asked Rita to move from Portland to Ashland as a favor. She was his final hope that one of his inner-circle friends could lead the Foundation. He didn't want to hire an outsider to fix the financial stress and political drama they were always in. Rita was his primary confidante other than his wife Nancy—his protector, promoter, and booker of all his speaking engagements. His wish was her next task—unless she was out on the golf course. Her loyalty was returned with even grander loyalty.

Every volunteer would eventually hear of the dramatic story in which she was the central character. On one of Rita's visits to Neale's home, they had an open fire set up outside the house for entertaining. Later that day Neale and family had a gathering in town, and she stayed back alone before preparing to go into town herself. When Neale returned home, the house was ablaze and the sky amber. Rita had forgot to put the fire out. Their relationship over time had withstood fires and a lot of people coming and going. She was like a grandfather clock in his life: sturdy, elegant, consistent—and always in Neale's corner.

Neale arrived at Rita's office first that Wednesday afternoon. The fluorescent lights were off and the blinds mostly closed. The darkness of the room matched the energy I felt as I arrived.

"Come on in," Rita said, sitting behind her large mahogany desk, which was clear of any papers. I took the only place left available—on the far end of a dark green three-seater couch where Neale was already leaning back.

Rita started in with an unsettling tone. "Neale has an issue with you that he would like to clear. He'll first share and then you'll have a chance to respond. I'll moderate, making sure you take turns and clearly hear where the other person is coming from."

I kept my gaze focused on Rita, who looked as solemn as I felt. I sat firm and leaned forward. My heart quickened at the sound of the word "clear."

The Foundation "clearings" were infamous. The initial intention of these forums was for people to share unresolved issues with each other so they wouldn't fester and create behind-the-back gossip or triangulation. Sometimes they worked, but often they became a platform to unleashed pent-up emotion and drama. The intention usually started off well-meaning, as everyone who worked there had good intentions. These clearings came from the genuine underlying desire to live the principles of CWG in the workplace. However, they could go on for hours or sometimes days in a row. We'd sit in our circle format with quotes from Neale's books behind us on the wall. No work would get done during these clearings, and often the entire staff, including volunteers who didn't have a clue what was going on, had to attend. In the beginning I didn't mind getting away from data entry for a day to watch an entertaining show of emotion, politics, and resolution. Later on, it got a bit tiresome.

No one had ever wanted to clear with me, but now I was with the boss, my favorite author, the facilitator I looked up to, and the man who intimidated me the most (even though I tried to hide that) and who never seemed to want to speak to me.

I took the deepest breath I could. "Okay, I'm here to be present and hear what you have to share," I said, doubting that my twentysomething insecurity would be any match for his fiftysomething experience and his title of "World-renowned Spiritual Teacher."

I turned to look at him and was met with a half-shut pensive gaze, calm behind his wire-framed glasses.

"I know you don't like me," he declared in a quiet voice.

Silence.

I couldn't react quickly enough to respond, as this was the last thing I expected him to say.

"After all the opportunities that I have given you, I don't understand why you treat me the way you do."

Stunned silence on my part.

Neale continued. "You never come up and talk to me. You never approach me with a hug. Everyone else in the organization does but you."

More silence from me.

I was shocked by what I considered his vulnerability. I still didn't know how to respond. I had never seen a side of him that wanted my approval, though I'd always wanted his.

My confused silence agitated him, and he shifted gears in an instant. As his volume increased, I was now on the receiving end of superiority rather than vulnerability. "You don't treat me with the respect that I deserve. You think and act like you are above me, and you are not."

The reverberations of his angry voice made me defensive, and I responded as politely as I could. "I have never felt that you wanted a hug from me. I don't ever get the feeling that you want me to talk to you. I thought you just wanted me to leave you alone and do my thing. I do respect you, Neale; I'm sorry you don't feel that."

He sat forward. "No, you don't. You don't give me the respect I deserve. I know you have done amazing things for this Foundation, but I am still the one who created this whole thing."

The tear I was trying to hold at bay eventually ran down my cheek for Neale and Rita to witness. He softened as I broke down.

"Look, my dear," Neale said, reverting to his gentle self in an instant. "Let's shift the way we work together."

"Okay," I said, sounding a lot like my inner five-year-old girl.

"What can you shift on your end?" he inquired with what seemed like love in his eyes.

"I will do my best to come and give you a hug and talk to you more," I said, sounding more like a question than a statement.

"That would be nice," he replied.

"I will ask you more questions when we need to make a big decision about the program," I continued, not knowing if he really wanted that.

"That would be nice also."

Whatever he said after that didn't penetrate. I was emotionally overloaded. The room felt darker. The Roman numerals on the wall clock behind Rita were no help, as I wanted time to speed up so I could disappear.

Neale stood up first. He offered his arms. I gave half of myself to his hug and walked out of Rita's office numb. I packed up my soft-shell briefcase with papers from the day and went straight home. I walked straight up the stairs and fell facedown on my bed. I didn't eat dinner. Not even chocolate chip cookies. I didn't show my face until morning.

I was ashamed that Neale was unhappy with me. I wasn't being a good girl for the teacher. Neale had changed my life, as he'd changed millions of lives. I'd left my homeland to dive into his teachings. His work gave me a deeper spiritual understanding and a greater awareness of who I was. He gave me a chance to learn from his masterful skills as a facilitator. His work gave me a visa and a place to stay.

When Neale led retreats, he did so with a magnanimous desire to serve others. Few could match his mastery at conducting an intervention when someone took the microphone and shared their story. I was devastated by his accusations.

Did he really care about what I thought of him?

That day in Rita's office helped me rethink how I judged intense personalities. Everyone has a scared little boy or girl inside them.

By drowning in my own vulnerability that night, I realized why he thought I didn't like him. While hearing Neale's grievance, I was too busy feeling defensive, but he was right. I didn't like him. I respected his position as an author and leader of the CWG movement, but he could shift from ascended master to angry quicker than anyone I'd seen. I wasn't accustomed to being around people who were so quick-tempered and experts at making others feel stupid. He was one of the most intuitive people I had ever met, and he had correctly sensed that I didn't like him.

This realization humbled me. I was being judgmental. By seeing myself as superior, I made myself feel better about my fears. The darkness of Rita's office, the unexpected reprimand, and my judgment of him invited me to embrace the ugliest side of myself. I felt sick realizing I was "spiritually arrogant." This was the first time I found myself in the eye of the storm, which I now call "Integrating Your Shadow." I felt ugly. Worse than that, my ugliness had been seen—by someone I never wanted to see it.

CHAPTER 15

THE GURU CHAIR

I was excited and happy to be journeying to England with Neale to support one of his two-day trainings there. His fourth marriage had recently ended, and his new romantic partner, Young Hee, and I were the only ones accompanying him on that trip. I was to handle the registration of the 50 attendees as well as making sure the chairs, tissues, and water were in the right places while Young Hee attended to Neale.

I enjoyed all the trainings I helped organize, especially because I received the lessons for free and traveled to new places. This role allowed me to sit in the back of the room and watch a master in action. I started to see patterns in the ways Neale brought people into their bodies, then into their emotions, then into greater awareness of why their life was the way it was. At times Neale used no strategy, only presence. He would listen to an audience member for minutes on end with the stillness and focus of a patient Buddhist monk. He could easily tune back into the Source that spoke to him when writing his books. From that place, the most intuitive insights about the person in front of him would flood out of him. I wanted to be able to do that.

Leading up to the trip to England, Neale fell ill. He could barely move by the end of day one, when he called me to his hotel room.

"I need to rest. Do you think you could lead the group tomorrow?" he inquired.

"Ah, I guess," I uttered with trepidation, not sure if Neale really knew what he was asking me to do.

Everyone expected to see Neale the next day. They had paid to hear the seven-times *New York Times* best-selling author and world-renowned spiritual teacher, and now he was proposing that they be led by the young woman in charge of the Kleenex.

All the attendees but one were older than me—most by a good 20 years. Experience had shown me people weren't usually eager to hear wisdom from someone half their age. Mostly I was scared, but I felt an inner stillness and knew I could handle it, as I'd heard Neale talk about the concepts I needed to present dozens of times.

Neale did not have the energy to give me any advice. He pushed himself up out of his chair and walked behind the wall divider of his hotel suite and lay down on the bed. Young Hee walked me to the door and gave me her sweet Korean smile that said *You can do this.*

I prepared for an hour that night. Before I slipped into bed, I walked to the window and peered down. I loved seeing the red double-decker buses passing each other in the street and cars half the size of American vehicles. I cracked open the wood frame, and the atmosphere was surprisingly quiet. *In another foreign land pushing up against my comfort zone again,* I thought.

I woke up with a nervous roiling in the pit in my stomach. In my mind's eye I saw disappointed and disgruntled faces staring at me as they realized their spiritual leader would not appear. I knew most of them would judge me as a poor substitute for the man who spoke to God. They would probably demand their money back. I couldn't blame them.

I walked into the room that morning thinking *Fake it till you make it.* My shoulders were thrust back and chin arched higher than usual. After greeting several of the participants, I announced, "We'll be starting in two minutes, please take your seats." I walked to the front of the room and stared at what I called "the Guru Chair." Neale always sat in a big lounge chair on a slightly raised platform. Its soft velvet upholstery beckoned me. I wanted to be propelled by its magic. All the same, I couldn't help thinking I was going to look like a tiny koala sitting on a large sofa.

I turned to face the audience, who appeared confused that I was standing in front of Neale's throne, and invited everyone to be silent with their emotions and intentions for the day. This gave me time to calm my nerves as I sat down and got comfortable with my back now cushioned in the Guru Chair. I needed more quiet time before I felt confident enough to share my opening remarks, including the bad news. In the stillness, I felt the impulse to use the fact that Neale wasn't present as a practice of awareness—for everyone to notice how they respond when they are disappointed that someone did not show up for them.

"Neale is unwell and apologizes that he cannot be here today."

The initial expressions were of concern.

"It's nothing too serious or life-threatening, but he needs at least a few days to rest," I stated, trying to sound 10 years older and completely in control of the situation.

The next set of expressions were concern for themselves. *Who's going to lead us today?* I imagined them all wondering.

"I will be the one to lead you through the material today. Plus, I have a series of practices I think you'll find very useful for your awakening journey."

No one wanted to hear that. My best attempt at authority and enthusiasm fell flat. Still, in the awkward silence, I felt some of the audience getting over their disappointment and starting to feel sorry for me.

I had prepared an opening statement, but its contents now eluded me. Instead, words I had not planned came out of my mouth.

"What usually happens when you get dealt a hand that you were not expecting?"

Pregnant pause.

"Take a moment to think about that. Do you blame, do you get angry, or do you draw the conclusion that you have missed out on something and it's not fair? What usually is your first and most immediate reaction?"

They all looked at me while pondering those questions. No one smiled.

"Your reaction to what happens in these scenarios will tell you a lot about why your life is the way that it is," I continued. "It doesn't matter to me how you reacted to the news about Neale not being here and instead you get me—and yes, I know some of you are thinking, *How old is she, anyhow?* What matters right now is whether you can be open to this being one of the most profound days of your life."

Those words felt exhilarating to me.

I opened the floor for people to share their honest reaction to my substituting for Neale and how that reaction related to their mental habits. After a few shares, the group felt connected again. I set up a process I had chosen the night before that suited my comfort level. As I sat back on the raised platform and observed everyone, now paired up, facing each other, and talking, I started to see the matrix again that connects us all, the same one I first saw at Satina's house years ago. I could visually see how and why one woman was "triggering" another woman and how they had made a spiritual agreement to meet there and work through it. I could see a short man with a large nose irritating and turning off everyone around him without knowing why. I could see his entire history and why he did what he did. Later in the day, a physically strong man in his mid-forties tried to defend me when someone gave me a tough question in a patronizing tone. I gently showed him that he had a pattern of overprotection and assured him I didn't need a shield. I felt a force behind my eyes, looking out and seeing patterns everywhere. I thought, *This must be the state known as flow.*

The short man who'd been irritating everyone became more disruptive. He kept over-sharing and giving advice when it was not welcome. He had now ostracized himself from the entire room. It's hard to describe, but I felt his soul talking to mine. It was saying, "You have permission to bring this to his attention in this room, right now, in front of all these witnesses. Part of him does not understand why he's never been able to receive the love that he desperately craves. Today you can help him heal that pattern."

The man wasn't giving me permission at all. I'm sure he was grumbling, *What can this girl tell me that I don't already know?* But my soul was saying, "Go for it. The time is now. You are the conduit for this breakthrough. Please help him."

What was opening this channel for clear sight? I didn't know.

I waited for the right opportunity for the intervention. I knew it would come. We gathered in one big circle late that afternoon, and as we were wrapping up before our final dinner break, a woman shared an experience that really struck an emotional chord with the rest of the room. She opened everyone's hearts with her tenderness. Then, right on time, this man interjected a piece of unwanted advice, and everyone's eyes rolled back in their heads. I saw the opening and ran straight into it.

"May I ask you a question?" I posed.

He just looked at me with a confused expression.

"Do you sometimes feel that you push people away from you?" I continued.

He thought about it and eventually nodded. His bravado abandoned him as all eyes locked on his face.

"Do you know why?" I asked, getting quieter with each syllable.

He took what felt like an eternity to look around at the group that had rejected him. "I'm not exactly sure why. I know I repel a lot of you."

I saw a few mouths in the audience start to open and help out. "Shhh! Don't anyone else say a word here."

I tried to ask my next question with the tenderness of a nurse before an anxious patient's surgery. "Do I have your permission to share why this might be happening?"

He was startled that I had the guts to ask him that. "Yes," he said, shifting in his seat.

Every time I have facilitated since that day I've always checked in as to whether the person in front of me has given me permission to intervene—either verbally or on a Soul level. If they have not, I know there will be resistance and the intervention is not going to end well. I have also learned that before telling anyone anything that might be hard for them to hear, I should always assess how much love I feel for them in that moment. If I am not in love with the person, I should keep my mouth shut. If they feel anything but full acceptance of who they are, they will not receive what I have to say. They have to feel total non-judgment.

It was easy for me to love this man. He was adorable in his own way. He acted like a little kid in a short man's body who had never received the love or discipline he needed to function well in a relationship. He had searched for the answer through spirituality. He had attended more spiritual workshops than most but would consistently push everyone away. I told him everything I saw in him. I told him, "Your soul brought you here for this particular retreat with this group for us all to hold you in love so you can change this pattern."

I turned to the rest of the group, as many of them were pissed at him for interrupting their training.

"You brought him here. Why did you bring him here?"

I paused.

"You all brought him here to love more unconditionally. Do you see the boy inside this man? Those who cannot yet feel the love for this adorable man right now, look at him. Who in your life are you doing this to? Who in your life are you judging and pushing away when they are aching for your attention and love?"

The tension dissipated. The boy within the man softened before our eyes. Compassion expanded. I invited the man to sit next to me in the circle. We talked, we processed, and he experienced an energetic shift inside him that switched him from repelling everyone to attracting everyone. We held hands and everyone in that room received some measure of blessing that day.

I had received the greatest one of all. I was thrown into the deep end that day and found that I could swim. For the first time

I directly experienced the magic that was possible as a workshop facilitator and I wanted more. I was reminded of a Rumi passage that night:

Everyone has been made for some particular work,
and the desire for that work has been put in every heart.

This experience propelled me to spend countless hours working on my craft as a coach, teacher, and facilitator. Any chance Neale gave me, I took. Any chance I could create for myself, I did. The next time the CWG Education Program traveled to England, Neale did not need to go. I had found my wings.

An "Angel Wash" is a group experience where everyone takes their turn to walk in the middle of two lines of people blindfolded and receive messages of appreciation and acknowledgment for who they are. My co-leader and I decided to end the final night of the training in London in this way. As soft music, gentle hugs, and whispers infused the room, I couldn't help but notice the contrast between what we had created and the emergency sirens that rushed down the street. They were continuous for what seemed to be a half hour.

When we were almost finished with the Angel Wash, one of the hotel managers walked through the candlelit room and whispered in my ear the startling message, "A bomb has just gone off at the local train station."

Weeks before, on the morning of Thursday, July 7, 2005, four Islamist extremists had detonated three bombs in quick succession aboard underground trains across the city, and later, a fourth on a double-decker bus in Tavistock Square. Fifty-two people were killed and over 700 more were injured in the attacks, making it Britain's deadliest terrorist incident since the 1988 bombing of Pan Am Flight 103. These attacks were fresh in the minds of everyone in the room and had stopped others from attending the training. There I was, in the center of a loving experience, while at the same time less than two miles away, I was told a horrific act of hatred had taken place.

I was struck by the polarity of life. No matter how much love you embody and emit, it doesn't make bad things disappear. I'd heard Eckhart Tolle explain on multiple occasions that even when you reach transcendence or enlightenment, there will still be challenges. However, you won't ever need to suffer through them because you don't react in fear and judgment; instead, you respond with presence and love. This helped me come to terms with the violent images that flooded into my mind's eye.

We ended the training that night in a circle, holding hands, with sirens still screaming by. No one but me, the hotel manager, and my co-leader knew what had happened just down the road. I closed with how proud I was of the group and grateful for the love that was shared.

"It is time to take that love out into the rest of your lives," I told them. "It's easy to be full of love in here, but when things happen out there, it's easy to shut down and go back into fear," I said. "There is always polarity in life. CWG calls it 'The Opposite.' That is what is happening right now."

I paused and dropped my attention and breath to my belly.

"I was just told by one of the managers that a bomb just went off at the closest station to where we are. We can take this situation as a call to something greater. We can choose to not go into fear and instead stay in love and share our love. We can be part of the solution and not the problem. Please stay safe. Please check with the hotel front desk about what's happening if you are leaving on public transport tonight. Finally, allow me to leave you with Rumi. Take his words with you, as tomorrow is another opportunity to be who you really are.

> *Today like every other day, we wake up empty and frightened.*
> *Don't open the door to the study and begin reading.*
> *Take down a musical instrument. Let the beauty we love be what we do.*
> *There are hundreds of ways to kneel and kiss the ground.*

When Grace is present in us, it lowers all resistance to the next inevitable challenge. I try not to pray as much to stop bad things from happening because sometimes they turn out to be gifts. Instead I pray that I have the wisdom to stop calling something bad just because it feels challenging at the moment.

I found out the next morning that it was only a bomb threat and no one was hurt. I left for Heathrow grateful for that and grateful that the right words had poured out of me at the right time. When I was put into a circle of people ready to do their "deep work," I could somehow circumvent my left brain and speak from a whole new depth.

Unfortunately, as much as my heart was in the right spot, finding this new skill of being in a flow state with a Higher Power while facilitating and leading the transformational experiences created fertile soil for my spiritual arrogance to grow—which would get me in trouble again sooner rather than later.

CHAPTER 16

MY SHADOW OF ARROGANCE

I began seeing my path stretched out in front of me. I wanted to be an inspirational speaker and facilitator who could stand in front of a room and create a magical experience for everyone who was open to it. I wanted to feel the empowered state of sharing my wisdom without hesitation or apology. I had wanted this for many years but was more often in the shadow of Neale and the other facilitators I would bring in to facilitate parts of the Leadership program.

On the other hand, this vision of my potential self frightened me. Judgment from others scared me the most. *What would others think if I said this? How would others react if I did that?* Of all the words in the English dictionary, the one I most didn't want anyone to call me was "arrogant." I know most people don't want to be judged as arrogant, but I disliked it more than most.

Deeply embedded into the Aussie culture is what is known as the "Tall Poppy Syndrome." If you grow too tall—meaning taller than the other poppies—you need to be cut down to size. The culture promotes humility with no bragging. If you do eventually excel at a pursuit, you better not think you are "all that" because if you do, someone will cut you down to size.

People had seen the arrogant side of me before. In my teens, even though I thought I was being very sweet and non-judgmental, friends sometimes commented on how I thought I was better than them. Even my mum, the person I most respected, found a politically correct way to tell me I was becoming too full of myself. That happened after I started to talk to her about spiritual things over our morning scrambled eggs and newspapers. At the time she, too, was finding a new understanding of God in the modern world. I loved our deeper conversations, and I felt at the time our dining table debates were a way to connect more as equals. She felt, however, that I was trying to show how superior I was in my understanding. It was never my conscious intention, but in hindsight I see that was exactly what I was doing.

Eventually I saw I was indeed judging others for being less aware, which came across as arrogance. In my early twenties, Debbie Ford's book *The Dark Side of the Light Chasers* showed me what happens when you put a part of your personality in the dark shadows of your unconscious. Others can see that "Shadow Part," but you cannot. One day I asked myself, *Why have I created this pattern in which people call me arrogant when it is the last thing I am trying to be?* My answer came in an unlikely form.

Our annual staff retreat for the Foundation that year, held in Neale's home, was facilitated by Tej Steiner, a master in group dynamics. With his long hair pulled back into a ponytail, piercing eyes, neck beads, and sandals, he took his spirituality seriously. I'd met Tej two years prior and spent many hours in circles with him. He was becoming my most treasured mentor. He knew both my potential and my shortcomings well.

I was excited to get out of the office and dive deeper into personal intentions for our individual lives and our camaraderie as a team. During the retreat, each one of us had a chance to share what we wanted for the upcoming year that would bring us more joy and expansion.

When my turn came, I launched into sharing my vision with the utmost conviction in my voice and gestures. "I feel there is a whole other level we can take this Leadership Program to. I want to be the one to bring in even better teachers, ones who are world-class at teaching their subject matter. Given the reputation Neale and the Foundation have, I think we could attract the top-level trainers in the world. I want to learn from the best and I want to coordinate this so we can all benefit from these teachers as we support them and our clients in the back of the room. I'm so excited by this idea. I want to learn from the best."

I took a breath and let in how proud I was for this desire and how I could see this vision coming to fruition. As my eyes came into proper focus, I looked around the room at my colleagues and friends. Every one of them wore a deadpan face. No smiles, no support, no enthusiasm.

Tej turned to the circle, who all sat on floor chairs or yoga bolsters, with a single candle burning in the middle. "Do not go by her words but instead her energy, and feel whether this is her heart's deepest desire."

I was grinning like a Cheshire cat, waiting to be fed with praise and agreement. Instead every single one of the group said, "No."

Tej stepped in. "Do you know why they are all saying that they don't feel your desire?"

"I have no idea," I answered with a frown.

"Does anyone want to share why they feel it's not her deepest desire?"

Julia took the baton. "I know you have done a great job to put this program together, but I don't feel you are happy being in the back of the room helping others shine in front."

I was totally caught off guard.

"What do you mean?" I asked innocently.

Tej interjected. "Can you close your eyes for a moment and again feel in your heart what would bring you the most joy and expansion?" He paused and waited.

I took a deep belly breath and looked inward.

Tej kept leading me with his gentle voice. "Just stay curious about this question: what am I wanting at the deepest level that will make my soul feel good?"

After a few minutes of silence and steady breathing, the answer came. I knew I hit on something because of the quickening of my heart and the speed that tears were now filling my closed eyes. Without opening them, I risked sharing my desire.

"I want to be the one in the spotlight." My voice creaked like an old hinge resistant to opening. "I want to be the one teaching and facilitating and not just organizing the events behind the scenes."

I opened my eyes, and almost everyone in the circle was smiling and nodding. "As I feel your support and smiles here, I feel safer to share with you how much I love teaching and feel I have the talent for being an excellent speaker and facilitator. I want to find every opportunity to excel at this." My voice quavered with insecurity, but I was relieved that I finally had stated something I had kept buried.

My declaration was supported by all but two people in the room. Another one of those "clearings" that I loved so much was ignited. Two of the senior staff members also wanted the same thing and were triggered. Both women had been my mentors and supervisors. They both took their turn to share how arrogant I was to essentially say I was going to be the best facilitator on staff. I was at least 10 years—and in some cases 20 years—younger than everyone else on the leadership team. I had been there the shortest period of time by far, and I was excelling in my role at a very high level.

Even though I believed some of their anger stemmed from their own insecurities and that they had misrepresented what I said, I could tell part of this dynamic was tied to a force I possessed that was eliciting this reaction. Others had called me arrogant to my face many times.

At the end of the day, exhausted and almost in tears, I asked Tej, "Why do they think I'm arrogant? Both of these women have said things like this to me in the past."

He opened the sliding glass door and stepped me out onto the cool grass outside. He then said something I never would have expected.

"They are reacting to you this way because you are not being arrogant when you should be."

"What? I don't understand." I thought he must have said it the wrong way around.

"It's not because you are being arrogant; it's because you are not being arrogant when you should be."

My eyebrows found new ways to crinkle. My face found new ways to contort.

"This is going to confuse you for a moment, but stay with me," he said. "You are excelling at what you are doing. You are in many ways doing a much better job than anyone here. If you owned that fully, they would own it. You are not fully owning your brilliance, because at the same time you are trying to be humble. The result is that you don't really claim the power that you own, which sends mixed signals."

A dim light turned on in my head, but I still had to sleep on the concept. I couldn't comprehend it in a single conversation. I steeped in the explanation for a few days and gradually the light grew brighter. Months would pass before I fully realized it. Those who own that they are better at certain things make it easy for others to allow the truth of that. I had one foot in and one foot out. The one foot in declared I was kicking ass in front of the room with the expanded spiritual awareness I had gained. The foot that was out was saying, "But I'm not any better than any of you at this, since you have been here so much longer." The polite Australian girl in me was trying to quash the part of me that knew I was born for this and loved every moment of it. Their reaction to me had little to do with my age, but everything to do with my lack of owning my power.

Being caught in the fear that others would think I was arrogant made it impossible for me to harness the helpful energy I needed to become a leader.

I began asking myself the question, "What is the energy within arrogance that could help me if I wanted to be an inspirational speaker and teacher?"

Eventually, I realized it was the energy of conviction and owning that I really knew my topic. I could honor that I had a greater level of awareness and mastery with some of the things that I was teaching than most people. I will always remain a student on the path to greater mastery, but once I realized and could own that I was better at what I was teaching, I could harness that empowerment fully. I didn't need to speak in a nice, polite way, wanting everyone to feel that they were all on the same level as me.

I didn't want anyone to think I was too full of myself, but politeness was holding me back in my presentations. I couldn't create the huge breakthroughs in people that I wanted. I wanted to strike a nerve. I wanted to push people's boundaries and shake things up, but I couldn't do that while being a good girl. I've never thought I was inherently better than anyone else and that somehow I was a superior being. I'm not. I don't believe that at all. I had to go to the edge of my comfort zone and identify a part of me that was confident. As I became more aware of this Shadow Part of myself, I started to own my mastery in certain areas. Teaching from that place made me far more effective and way more magnetic to the audiences I wanted to attract. The most surprising by-product was that no one called me arrogant anymore. I was getting more edgy and unapologetic by the day, and people loved it. What a paradox!

As I slipped my shoes off to ground myself in the damp grass outside Neale's door that day, I was taking the first steps in opening up to my Shadow. Just as when Neale confronted me in Rita's office, I was disgusted to acknowledge the ugliest parts of myself, but it ultimately felt so good to do so.

Arrogance was the first big Shadow for me. It was very difficult to accept the part of me that was arrogant. I have since created a practice called Shadow of the Month. Each month my clients and I pick a quality that feels uncomfortable to acknowledge, own, or express. I started to see it at work, but it was my Shadow in romance that was yet to fully rear its ugly head so I could stare it in the face.

CHAPTER 17

THE RETURN

Subject line: Hi there

Hi Rach,

I hope you are doing well. Things have been interesting here.

Rachael is pregnant. The relationship has been very challenging. She is not sure if she is having the baby yet, but I am ending the romantic relationship. I'm doing my best to stay present with it all.

I miss seeing you. Would you like to catch up?

Robert

I read it several times to make sure I was reading it clearly. My mouth opened and my heart raced. My first thought was, *This time I'm very glad to be the other Rachael.*

That could have been me. I'd never wanted to have children, though not because I don't like them. I've just never felt the impulse inside me. Plus, the first time I saw a birthing video in the mandatory high school class, I fell off my science lab stool and passed out, lucky to not get a concussion. That was enough for me. I always thought I might partner with someone who already had kids, but that is the only way I wanted them to enter my life. I didn't want to get pregnant. I didn't want to go into labor. I couldn't have been more sure.

I couldn't focus on work for the rest of the day as I drafted six different responses in my head. I sensed his email was a confirmation of sorts: showing up seven days too late a year ago was a lucky break, contributing to my highest good. But no matter how much I tried to be practical, I could not get this unyielding thought out of my head. *Is this an opening for the love that was supposed to be ours?*

If I had been a more mature, level-headed woman I might have declined the request, but instead I found myself typing;

> I don't really know what to say. I'm sorry it's been challenging.
> Yes, I'd love to catch up.
> Love Rach

The bells attached to the front door of the coffee shop jingled, and I looked up from my copy of *Vogue*. Robert walked in looking exhausted. Robert dated Rachael, got her pregnant, and the relationship fell apart. They weren't soul mates after all, and I felt less rejected and vulnerable. I stood and gave him a short hug, eager to tell him how fantastic things were going for me and how sorry I was for him. I still felt I had to redeem myself after his rejection. His stubble revealed more gray, and the lines under his eyes displayed his weariness. He'd lost weight.

Rachael had still not decided whether she was going to have the baby, and that was weighing on him. We caught up on the past year and acted like friends, though some of our chemistry returned. I was uncomfortable because it was too soon to do anything about the tension, and in my mind the purity of our connection had been tainted. Was I going to be the rebound woman after the most painful rejection of my life? I didn't want that—yet a part of me wanted exactly that.

With each meal and music act we saw together over the next few months, there was more hope, more accidental touching, more subtle flirting. Eventually the vision of a full life together returned to the canvas of my imagination.

The return of Robert to my life was a final confirmation that I was going to stay in America for good. I hired an immigration attorney out of Portland. My career was about to take off, and my love life was showing promise. Finally!

Then came the blow. Discovering the process I had to go through to get an employment visa and then a green card was devastating. I learned I had to find a company to sponsor me and confirm that I had the equivalent to a four-year bachelor's degree in my chosen industry. Plus, I had to prove that no American citizen was available and qualified for the job.

My bachelor's degree was in music business, which had nothing to do with organizing and teaching spiritual development, and there were many Americans who wanted to do precisely that. To throw another wrench in the works, I didn't want the sponsoring company to be the Foundation, as my divinely inspired desire to finish with them and do my own thing got stronger by the day. I had to find someone who had never hired me before to go through a six-month procedure to hire me—all the while persuading them to allow me to run my own business on the side. I had to somehow prove my university education related to the spiritual growth work I was doing now. This appeared to be an impossible order. As I contemplated the twenty rabbits I had to pull out of a hat, in a specific order and time frame, I couldn't help thinking that my lack of getting a visa on time was again going to be the reason that love would be taken away. I had to make this work.

I didn't want to go back to a country that had nothing for me. I couldn't see Melbourne as a fertile ground for the expansive life I wanted. My spirit sank into depression whenever I contemplated being forced to leave my home in Ashland, my friends, my career, my mentors, my spiritual community, and Robert. I started pleading with God and anyone else who would listen. *I don't want to go back. I can't go back. It will kill me.*

The phone rang. His smooth voice made me happy. "I'm in a good mood, and I want to go see some music tonight. Do you want to come?"

I never said no to him.

He picked me up in his Volkswagen, gave me a longer hug and a polite kiss on the cheek, and opened the car door for me. This scene had played out before, but this time the sizzle in his touch ran up and down my body in the best possible way. We ordered drinks at the bar, and when they arrived, he turned to me and with a charming smile delivered the news.

"Rachael has decided not to have the baby. I'm complete with her." He held my gaze, and for the first time since I left him at the airport I felt the energy from his eyes that he used to direct right into my heart.

"I know you would've been fine with whatever she decided," I said.

"For sure. I was ready for a child, but this is for the best."

"Let's toast to moving onward," I said, holding up my wine glass. The clink of the glasses left us in silence. The last few meetings we had mostly talked about Rachael, her decision, and how he was feeling about the unknown. Now that was settled.

He held my gaze without words. The electric surge between our bodies seated on the cushioned barstools was potent. The blues band behind us and the hum of the crowd seemed quieter. I blushed.

That night I invited him in to my home, to my room, and to my bed. It was the moment I had looked forward to, then lost sight of, and now it was happening. As he unbuttoned my blouse, I was nervous. As I lay on top of him I felt awkward. My body was uncooperative to our plans. I was rushing. I was hurting. I tried to slow time down. I wanted to look into his crystal-blue eyes again and feel the moment stand still. I wanted to become lost in his face and enraptured in the spiritual experience we had once shared together. As much as I wanted that right then, it did not happen that night. Time did not stand still. He left at midnight.

A few nights later, we went out for Middle Eastern food and I could feel heaviness in his heart again. "She is now not sure if she wants the baby or not. She keeps changing her mind," he said, dejected.

"Oh jeez," was the most supportive response I could muster. My happiness was on the line now too. I was caught up in their drama. I usually loved drama, as it gave my life significance, but this time it felt horrible.

He looked down at his lap and stated half-heartedly, "I can't let her decision hold me ransom. I have to let her make the decision and I'll deal with it day by day from there."

"I'll support you through this any way that I can," I said. "I'm here for you."

He looked up and gave his best attempt at a smile.

I cheered him up that night and gave him a taste of what was possible if he had me—full-time—in his life. I flattered him. I told him it was all going to work out for the best. We made love and the connection was stronger. He stayed in my bed half an hour longer this time.

I did my best to keep giving him space. I let him reach out and take the lead rather than my being the one to call most of the time. I was proud I had mastered the art of not trying too hard with the man you want. He still had a lot on his mind, so I didn't mind taking the leftover scraps of his time.

I practiced everything I had learned about manifesting miracles for hours every day. I was disciplined with the Law of

Attraction practices I learned from my hundreds of hours listening to Abraham-Hicks. One of their recordings was almost always playing in the background during my lonely moments. I would visualize a scene of me with Robert and hearing the news that my visa was renewed. I would feel elated; I would express gratitude for it already happening; and if I woke up in fear, I changed my emotional state within minutes.

From this intensity of practice, miracles around my visa application were being created and rabbits were jumping out of hats all over the place. The result was that my friend Paul from Toastmasters who ran CWG Coaching Services offered to sponsor me. I had helped him become an integral part of the CWG Leadership Program, and he saw ways I could help continue to support their business. We had a gentleman's agreement that I could stay working for CWG Foundation until I chose not to anymore. The Foundation would become a client of ours. I could work for Paul and his business partner Jim and create my own thing through their business. We found a creative and legal way to prove I'd had two years toward a bachelor's degree in the industry (I had studied social work right out of high school) and had at least four extra years in work experience, which made up for the other two years of a degree that I didn't have. Our lawyer felt confident with our approach but would not promise success. We completed hours of paperwork. We passed the timeline during which no other American applied for the position and continued what I called "Law of Attraction on steroids."

In the wait for my visa approval I had some intimate times with Robert, but his full attention wasn't on me. I could feel his lack of commitment, but I believed I could turn that around in time. *Most likely he doesn't want to enter into a permanent relationship until my visa is approved,* I thought. *It's also that he probably doesn't want to hurt Rachael's feelings too soon.* I felt he also needed some reassurance that I was not going to create a crazy lifestyle, become famous, and travel the world all the time—because he is a quiet, private homebody. Once the visa came through, I knew things would change.

The visa was not approved within the time frame they said. History was repeating itself. I had four weeks left until my current visa was up and I had to leave the country. Four weeks turned into three.

"This is crazy," I said to Paul. "Do I pack? Do I buy a plane ticket for Australia just in case? Do I start saying goodbye to all my friends?"

Three weeks turned into two.

Now I was certifiably freaked out. I did not want to go back. Was my life going to be ripped apart?

Two weeks turned into one week.

My lawyer made some calls to find out what was going on, and then she called me. "I can't promise a successful outcome and I don't know why it's being held up. You should start to make plans to leave the country just in case."

The Foundation ordered me to work from home, as Neale was concerned that someone would find out that they were housing an illegal alien, even though I wasn't illegal.

With two days to go and the pit in my stomach becoming a full-blown cavern of nausea, I opened up my email inbox and down dropped an email from my lawyer.

> Subject line: H1B Visa
> Hi Rachael Jayne,
> I just received word from the INS that your H1B visa has been approved.
> You will be receiving paperwork very shortly that you and Paul need to complete. There are a few more steps that we need to do together to finalize documents.
> It is with great joy that I can give you this news.
> Congratulations.
> Yours Sincerely,
> Raquel Hecht

Before I could process the last line of the email, a joyful cry emanated from my throat and echoed all over the house. I was thankful the other volunteers were all at the office. The shift from stress to relief was so great I cried on and off for hours. I called Paul, then Julia and the Foundation staff, and they could hardly understand me through the blubbering. They laughed at me because I couldn't talk properly. I have never in my life experienced such relief before or since.

I waited to call Robert. *How am I going to play this one?* I contemplated. If I was honest with myself, I was scared that he wasn't going to be ecstatic and that I would finally realize which way this relationship was going.

"I'm so happy for you, sweetie," was his response over the phone. He never gave away too much of how he felt. His version of excited was pretty subdued compared to mine. That was a challenge. I want to know how people feel. He was quick to detach from emotions, even though his energy felt open and kind. I often didn't know where I stood with him.

My new visa guaranteed me another three years in the States. Ten days passed until Robert had time to celebrate with me. I pretended I wasn't upset.

Another two weeks passed before he called me again, and that was torture. I continued to remind myself that I wasn't going to do any chasing. I was going to let him show me how much he was interested. Every time we met, he wasn't in his usual spirits. Or were they his usual spirits?

The silence was painful between our occasional rendezvous. His announcement was deflating: "She's having the baby." He was preparing to be a dad. "I'm so sorry I've been distant. I've been trying to process all of this. We are going to have to co-parent the best way we can, as I cannot be in a relationship with her."

He suspected she had some undiagnosed mental health issues. I'd never met her and didn't want to. I knew though the romantic relationship had ended with her, the cord would never be cut. His halfway presence with me was because of that, I would tell myself. I knew I had to be patient. I had all the time in the world now, so that's what I did. I was patient.

He found relief being with me. The occasional phone calls and nights together made me hopeful. But I never could recapture that excitement I had with him when we first met. It was not from lack of trying. He did not see me as his girlfriend, yet I still believed he was the one.

Hundreds of nights would pass when I would sit close enough to the phone while I watched TV so it would have no chance to go through to voicemail. He'd only call once every two weeks, sometimes longer. I put on weight. I cried a lot. I was not SINGLE and LOVING IT!

I prayed to God. I bargained with the Universe. "Please have him call me. I know that he is the one and I am the one for him. I promise to take great care of his broken heart. I can do that. I will make him happy again. Just please have him call me. Okay, let's get clear. I'm dying here. My heart is in so much pain. He is my man and he's not calling me. I know that no one else is such a good match for me. He is everything I want. I am ready for love. Please have him call me. I promise to support him through this challenging time. Love has been taken away from me too many times. Please don't let this one be taken away."

I would stare at the phone from across the living room, willing it to vibrate. It just remained a piece of machinery attached to the wall. It wasn't my friend that night. It wasn't my friend the next night, or the next.

Finally, the call came.

"Hi there," he spoke in his soft, gentle voice. It was still as sexy as ever, but these days his tone brought me more pain than pleasure.

"Hi, how are you?" I replied in an attempt to sound nonchalant.

"I'm doing pretty well." His usual response.

"That's good to hear," I said, patiently waiting to see if this call would lead to an invitation.

"How are you?"

"Doing great!" I lied.

"Would you like to go to the movies this weekend?"

"Yeah, I think that could work. What night did you have in mind?"

"Saturday night would work great for me."

The words *Saturday night* made me stand a little straighter as I held on to the phone that had betrayed me most nights. Saturday night meant it was a serious date. For a man like him, Saturday night was when you were with your special woman.

I took this as a good sign and started going through my wardrobe, prepping what I was going to wear. I would show him I was worth his attention. I promised myself that I would play this one differently. I started mentally preparing with my new game plan.

CHAPTER 18

LAPDOG

Robert rolled up in his new Subaru station wagon. With the trade-in of his hatchback I sensed his pride about becoming a dad. On this special Saturday evening I didn't follow my usual meet-and-greet habit, which consisted of me passing through the front door on the way to his car before he had a chance to knock on it. This time I waited. I'd let him come to me. From the window of my upstairs bedroom, with the lights off so he couldn't see me, I watched him get out of his car and make his way to the front door. The doorbell rang, and I waited a few extra seconds before heading downstairs. I wasn't going to appear too eager.

"You look great," he said.

I returned his compliment with a flirtatious smile. He didn't have to know I'd just spent 90 minutes on my makeup and hair. Or that I changed outfits six times before landing on a tight pair of black jeans, black heeled boots, and a fitted taupe button-up blouse that accented my red hair and cleavage just enough.

We made small talk on our way to the art-house movie theater. The smell of warmed popcorn filled the lobby as movie buffs selected their sugar high for the night. We looked at the prints encased on the wall for the upcoming movies and shared which ones we wanted to see. We took our seats in the third back row, and I felt excited to sit next to him again. His presence soothed my impatience. It was the night for things to turn—in our favor. The memory of him offering his hand in this same movie theater two years ago was in the forefront of my mind.

As the trailers ended and the feature film *Finding Neverland* began, I watched out of the corner of my eye for him to lift his hand. I knew it would come any moment and didn't want to miss it. The storyline deepened. No hand yet. The stakes got higher on-screen. No movement. I couldn't concentrate fully on the movie because I didn't want to miss his move. I wanted him to know I wanted to take his hand. I waited an hour and 32 minutes for his hand to lift from the shadows of his lap, but it never moved.

I had been in a casual dating relationship with him for 12 torturous months. His unavailable hand and the contrast of his willingness to sleep with me later that night were enough to start the onslaught of anger towards myself. *You are pathetic. You've made this all up. He doesn't love you. You are not the one for him! You are chubby. You are desperate. You are not the one he wants!*

The voice was right. I was not the strong, independent, self-assured woman I projected to others. I was attempting to hold on to something that didn't exist anymore. I was putting up with scraps. I should have yelled, "You are pathetic!" in the mirror months ago to wake myself up.

The emotional roller coaster had to end. I knew the only way that was going to happen was to totally cut off any connection with him. Otherwise, he'd keep pushing through the partly opened door whenever he felt like it. That would just keep me guessing and hoping.

I made the phone call 12 hours after the movie ended.

"I need to talk to you today. It's really important, and it needs to be in person. What time can I come over?" He had never heard me this forthright before, and the power in my voice put him on edge.

"How about in two hours?" he offered.

"I'll see you then." I hung up the phone with force, hoping that if I hit the receiver hard enough, I wouldn't change my mind about going through with this.

He had just moved. He now had a picket fence, an oak tree in the front yard, and a porch swing. It was gorgeous, and it would never be mine. He poured me a glass of water and I responded with cold silence. I sat down on his couch and without small talk made my declaration. "I'm not doing this any longer. I cannot see you anymore." He was surprised at my conviction, as he had recently asked me if I wanted to go away for a trip up the coast next month. "I'm ready for a long-lasting, committed love and I thought that could be with you, but I now know that it can't. I have to end this relationship in order to move on."

He looked down through the glass-top coffee table, trying to figure out how to respond. "Can we stay friends at least?" he asked. He wanted the door to stay open enough to get his foot in.

"No. I cannot see you for a very long time. I don't mean for a few months. I mean years. It's too hard."

"Should I at least email you in a few months to see how you are?" he asked.

"No." I was resolute.

My yearning in the movie theater had been too pathetic for me to ever go back to. I closed the door behind me and jumped into the rust bucket of a car that had originally transported me to this man in that bar two years earlier. I'd love to say that I looked straight ahead, started the engine, and drove off without hesitation. Not quite. I waited and stared through the rearview mirror at his front door. Just in case a dramatic Hollywood ending was coming where he'd rush out of the house, fall down on his knees, and declare that he'd been a fool. Instead, every second that passed screamed loudly in my ear that I'd been the fool. I drove away, never to return.

Why had I been such a lapdog for this guy? Why had I given so much time and energy to someone who gave me so little? Where had my fierce inner feminist gone? I succumbed to what I had promised I would never be—a woman willing to settle for a substandard relationship. As much as my compassionate heart understood my longing for love and how I could make naive mistakes, I had to admit to myself I was a fraud. I had not learned to love myself first. I had not yet learned to realize who people were and why they did what they did. I had not learned to trust that the deepest well of love would appear once I loved myself first and surrendered.

I went through a month of grief, clinging to the hope that closing one door would open another. My friend Ruthmary flew in from Montana for the first week to help me with the screaming, anger, and gut-wrenching sadness, and she came up with some creative ways to get my mind off things.

Ruthmary was Mum's age and I felt nurtured by her. She cooked for me and tucked me into bed every night for a week. She sat on the end of my bed and asked: "Have you ever been to a place and had such a good time that you went back again, but you didn't have as great of a time the second time?

"Yes, I guess so."

"That's normal, my dear. You went back hoping to get the same feeling back, but you couldn't. Don't beat yourself up for that. He was God's bait to bring you here. Look at your life now. This is where you are meant to be, and if you hadn't met him, you might not have fought so hard to come."

I had the blankets pulled right up to my chin. "But I wasted so much time on him. I didn't want to see the truth. I kept clinging to the idea that he was the one because I didn't believe that there was another man like him. At least not for me. I believed he was as good as it got." I slowly shook my head. "What a waste."

She saw my book of Rumi poems by Coleman Barks on my side table and flicked through the pages. She was also a fan, and it appeared she was looking for a particular passage. She found

"The Guest House" and said, "Close your eyes, my dear, and take this in."

> *This being human is a guest house.*
> *Every morning a new arrival.*
> *A joy, a depression, a meanness,*
> *some momentary awareness comes*
> *As an unexpected visitor.*
> *Welcome and entertain them all!*
> *Even if they're a crowd of sorrows,*
> *who violently sweep your house*
> *empty of its furniture,*
> *still treat each guest honorably.*
> *He may be clearing you out*
> *for some new delight.*
> *The dark thought, the shame, the malice,*
> *meet them at the door laughing,*
> *and invite them in.*
> *Be grateful for whoever comes,*
> *because each has been sent*
> *as a guide from beyond.*

He may be clearing me out for some new delight. That was the line that resonated the most.

On a late-night phone call from Mum, I was too emotional to have our usual catch-up conversation.

"I'm sorry I'm feeling emotional tonight. I just broke up with Robert."

"Oh darling, I didn't know you were back with him."

I was too ashamed to tell her it hadn't been a real relationship. I was so embarrassed about always being single.

"He wasn't treating me the way I needed."

She didn't know what to do with my tears from the other side of the world, but once she relapsed into silence, the words came. "That was a very wise thing to do, my dear. It is quite possibly the wisest thing you could ever do. You are one of the most passionate young women I know. Not many men will be right for you, but the one who is will treat you like you are the most treasured gift to him. When you find true love, there will be no doubt; there will only be full support. If someone cannot be that person easily—and live as if they were born to be your protector—then he is not the one for you."

Mum had never shared any relationship advice with me before. She didn't need to. She showed how it was done. Dad adored her, supported her, and protected her—there was no doubt. Mum was the glue in our family. She would call any of us kids if it had been too long. She filled us in with the celebrations and disappointments of both the immediate and extended family. Along with Rumi and Ruthmary, she was the glue that started to put the shattered pieces of my heart back in place that night. She could always make me feel loved when I needed it most.

CHAPTER 19

PRESENT WITH THE PAIN

For the next year I didn't believe anyone could measure up to Robert. My friends told me later they were reluctant to speak up about how they sensed he was a noncommittal drifter and how they didn't want to burst my bubble. I think my zealous conviction that he was the one led them to believe that it might work out. I felt some chemistry with a few men, which helped on my path of healing a hurt heart.

Jeff was one of them. He was the host of the local morning talk-back show on public radio and the author of several books. From the moment I saw him at my first softball game I could see he was the archetype of exactly what I wanted—and what a lot of women want. Tall, dark, handsome, smart, conscious, and masculine, he cared deeply for the environment and was a great listener. I'd always joked that I wanted to end up with someone who looked like Tom Selleck. Jeff could have been his brother—mustache and all.

He was a member of the board of directors at the Foundation and an intelligent advisor. He would drop in to the office and social gatherings on occasion and joined us for our four-day Warrior Monk training with Bill Kauth—which proved to be a massive distraction. While sitting in our sacred circle, burning sage to clear us each morning, reading Rumi, meditating, and observing silence at meal times, I felt anything but holy. I kept trying to steal glances at this hunk without anyone noticing. I couldn't keep my eyes off him. He was the epitome of magnetic. It probably never crossed anyone's mind that I had a crush on him, as he was 24 years older than me.

The Warrior Monk training included some deep process work, and we were asked to work in pairs a few times a day with different members of the group. On Day Three we were instructed on how to facilitate our partner in the most raw and vulnerable process of the retreat and asked to choose a partner we hadn't worked with yet. Jeff was standing in front of me within seconds. "We haven't worked together yet," he stated.

"No, we haven't."

Even if it had been an appropriate place to flirt, I would not have. I would have kept a straight face and tried to sound as smart as I could to somehow meet his Harvard graduate reputation. He was so out of my league.

We started the process together and both had intense releases of memories and emotion. I sensed that he didn't see me as a twenty-nine-year-old. We shared some sort of soul connection, however difficult to explain.

"You have a massive capacity to hold space for someone," he offered after a few hours had passed.

"Thank you," I said, nervously touching my forehead and not knowing what else to add.

Before we finished for that night, the group returned to the circle and I sat next to Jeff. The circle joined hands and my right hand was enveloped in his large, strong hold. We were connected for five minutes through meditation and closing remarks. I couldn't focus on anything but my hand in his. No candle, no incense, no prayer, no Rumi poem, just our two hands pulsing together. Finally, the circle broke and my hand felt weightless, then started to shake. I hid it as best I could. I ducked out of the retreat room before anyone else left that night and started my five-minute walk home under the night sky. My hand shook all the way home. I poured myself a chamomile tea, but my hand couldn't hold the mug still. I hoped I would fall asleep easily, but I just lay there awake, staring at the boring white ceiling with my right hand shaking out of my control.

Oh shit, what does this mean? I asked myself. I knew shaking was a sign for me, but a sign of what?

So began a respectful friendship and subtle spark between us that we never discussed. I'd run into him every few months, and every time we were in the same room I liked what I saw. Jeff had recently ended a relationship with a long-term girlfriend. I would've put my entire savings on never having a chance with him.

I joined a committee for the annual Ashland Christmas Swap, for which the community brought slightly used items that were swapped for others to use as gifts. Jeff was one of the founders of the idea, driven by his dedication to environmental causes and fighting unconscious capitalism. This led us to see each other more. He confided in me at times. He listened with presence when I shared my insights on the several issues he was having. Those conversations led to meeting for coffee, which led to seeing a few musical shows together, which led to some passionate making out in the front seats of my rust-bucket Chevrolet.

Jeff invited me over to his house for what he termed "a serious conversation" two days later. My pre-Robert history told me this probably meant it was over before it had a chance to get started. I sat on his big sofa in the open living area, and he sat on the other side of the coffee table. He had designed and built this gorgeous wood-frame and stone-floor oasis. Even his house was out of my league. Given the distance he put between us and his earnest expressions, I was prepared for the usual quick end to a relationship.

"I have been casually dating another lady over this past month. Over the last few days I've been doing some serious thinking about our relationship. I adore you and think you are one classy woman, so I don't want to just casually date you."

I kept my face bright, nodded attentively, and did my best to look detached while thinking to myself, *Go on; end it now. Just rip the Band-Aid off and let me leave.*

He continued, "I'm ready to break the other relationship off and commit to you. I feel this could be a significant relationship that meets my spiritual and physical needs. I want to have a relationship that I can commit to for the rest of my life, and I want that to be you. But I only want to move forward if you are ready for this and have thought through all the challenges of being in relationship with me."

The corner of my lips curled up and my body relaxed into the soft cushions behind me.

"Are you really okay with how much older I am than you?" he asked with concern. "Do you understand there will be talk around town once the news gets out and many people will judge me for this?"

That didn't faze me in the slightest.

"You will most likely be taking care of me in my older age; have you thought about that?" he asked. "Are you absolutely sure you don't want children?" he probed. "I don't want to have another relationship; I want this to be it. If you have any doubts about our different cycles of life we are in, I want to talk about that now."

I was being bombarded with questions from a man who also sought love. I had no doubts.

"I want this too. I have always felt our soul connection. I'm clear."

He came over to my side of the room and slid his wide fingers through my hair. "I'm so happy to hear this."

I knew my friends and others thought me naive. I knew they saw this as a short-lived romance, but they did not witness our commitment conversation, I told myself. I didn't care if they judged the age gap. I was always more comfortable with older men, as they were more evolved, more experienced, and more mature.

I had so much hope, yet within a week the energy between us had changed. I didn't know why. I felt my worst nightmare coming true. Again.

Three weeks later I stared, disillusioned, into Jeff's face, full of shame. Jeff was not finished with his ex-girlfriend. They'd rendezvoused behind my back, though to his credit he had the guts to tell me. He told me how sexually addicted he was to her. I had seen her perfectly tanned body, long caramel hair, and Sophia Loren eyes from a distance—I understood why.

He chose a walk along the bike track as the setting to tell me. "I'm so sorry. I still want to honor our relationship and give it some time. I'll understand if you don't want to."

"I need some time to think about all this," I said, feeling light-headed.

I wanted love more than anything. I wanted my man to be this man. Jeff was what I saw as the whole package. He wanted to be the chivalrous version of himself in this situation. I soaked in these questions for two days. *Can I forgive this indiscretion and march forward with commitment? Or is this someone I should not give any more of my time to?* We were friends. We had confided in each other. We loved each other.

I invited Jeff to join me at the hotel restaurant we were leading a seminar at. It was past dusk, and we tucked ourselves away in the corner to get some privacy. I looked squarely into his eyes, and even though I felt I was going to choke on my words, I spoke. "I want a man who looks deeply into my heart and soul and knows without a doubt that he wants to be with me."

The man sitting across the table was not that man—as much as we both wanted him to be. For the first time in my life I broke up with a man first. My maturity and self-worth won the battle for the first time in my life when it came to men. Even though I believed that perhaps no one better would come along, I was clear that I would no longer settle for less than what was right for me. I had to love myself more than love itself.

"Go back; finish things with her," I said, reaching out my hand to his as a gesture of how empowered I felt, even as I crumbled inside.

He was relieved by my answer. He was off the hook.

"You are an incredible and graceful woman. I am so sorry." He looked genuinely contrite. "I didn't mean to put you in this situation."

I knew he meant it, but that didn't offer me any relief.

My chest physically hurt as I watched him leave the restaurant. I made my way outside a few minutes later to get some fresh winter air. It was a few nights after Christmas and fairy lights were everywhere. Behind the building was a secluded open field that beckoned me to release my emotions in its embrace. My nose was red and my hands numb from the chill, but my inner body was a fiery ball of anger. Why was I deprived over and over again of love? Why did men want me in the beginning and so quickly change their mind? I looked up at the mountains and the full moon that illuminated the sky. My heart was overcome with terrible pain as I screamed from the depths of my gut. Then I heard that still, small voice say, *Don't ignore the hurt—feel it, from the depth of your being.* I felt pain, I felt anger, I felt betrayed. I felt like someone had wrenched my heart wide open. I kept groaning aloud with no fear of anyone hearing me, "WHY...WHY...Why does love always leave me?"

I leaned into the grief. I stayed embodied and present to the pain and to my heart's longing, desperately wanting to love and be loved by a strong man. I stretched my heart open with my arms out to my sides as the wind caressed my being. I breathed deep and screamed from all corners of my lungs. I stayed with the physical sensations and not my "story" of the event.

After what felt like ten minutes of staying with my discomfort, I was suddenly overcome with a sense of peace, then of deep love. For the first time in my life I met my pain head-on—with no resistance, no mental dialogue about what this meant—and moved through to the other side. I allowed the pain to open me, physically and energetically, and I was filled with love. I felt love for myself, love for Jeff, and love for all the men who had hurt me in the past. I felt love for the physical place where I was standing and for the moon above and the gravel beneath. Looking back, I see what an enormous signal I shot out into the universe that night: "I want a love relationship that has it all! I want a man who honors me." Through my pain my desire became clearer.

A few weeks later, one of Jeff's closest friends was found dead just meters off a local bike path. She was an adored masterful improvisational comedian that almost all the town had seen perform, and now she had taken her own life. The shock ripples were felt in many circles. I sat with hundreds of others at her memorial.

I hadn't seen Jeff since the hotel restaurant, so I asked Tej to sit with me for support. We took seats in the back. Then Jeff entered. He walked to the front with his model girlfriend by his side, and they took seats in the first row. Jeff's body looked like it had aged two years within two weeks. He seemed hunched over, his energy heavy.

Tej could feel Jeff's heaviness and mine—for different reasons. He caught me looking at the reunited couple and leaned over to whisper in my ear, "You need to be with a dancer. A man who dances through life."

I looked at him as if I didn't know what he meant.

"You deserve to be with a dancer. Don't you get that?"

After the service, Tej and I chose to let everyone leave first. I didn't want to risk bumping into Jeff. We leaned back in our chairs and took in the number of people who were in shock about this talented woman's choice.

"Tej, what if God wants me to be without a relationship for my whole life to learn a lesson? Maybe it's not in the cards for me," I said, hoping he would talk me out of my half-hearted belief.

"If you experience a strong heartfelt desire and you surrender to that, practicing profound patience, it will come. There are no lessons to learn. This deep love you want is coming to you.

Jeff is one of my best friends and I love him dearly, but I feel his energy. He's not a dancer. Your man is a dancer."

This rang true and offered relief to my aching heart.

• CHAPTER 20 •

EMBODIMENT

The search for true love became a doorway to spiritual realization. The lack of committed romantic love in my life was an impetus to grow. My pain beckoned me to go within and ask the important questions about who I was and how was I creating my reality. A new word that had started to pop into my awareness a couple of years before began to appear often, through books, workshops, and mentors.

That word was *embodiment*. At the time it wasn't a common word. I had the mental construct of what it meant, but I didn't have the physical and energetic experience of it.

Soon after my split from Jeff, while still in a whirlwind of confusion, I asked Tej to come to my office. I wanted the perspective of a man with whom I could be vulnerable.

He arrived with a tender hug, looked into my bloodshot eyes, and asked, "What's wrong?"

I closed the blinds for privacy. I fell into my office chair, pulled out another tissue, and planted my elbows on the desk and covered my face.

"Why does this keep happening? Why do these men seem so committed to me in the beginning, pretty much stating they want to spend the rest of their lives with me, and it doesn't hold for even a month? What am I not getting?"

Tej closed his eyes and breathed deeply. I did the same. We sat together in silence for a few minutes as we let the sounds of office workers pecking at computer keyboards in the next room fall away.

"They see something in you they want, then take it, and then they are gone," he said with precision.

"I don't feel like they are using me, though. I feel they truly love me in the beginning," I said defensively.

"I agree. I don't feel they are doing it on purpose or they are even aware of it. I have no doubt they are falling in love with you, but you are opening everything to them too quickly. You are getting swept away with their romantic notions of you, too. You have to be able to maintain your independence longer to see if they are worthy. You need to see if they are all talk, or if they fully join you."

This seemed to contradict past lessons. In the past I had felt guarded with men, and I thought to have more boundaries meant to be more guarded.

Tej, sitting in the corner chair across the room from me, explained: "It's not about going back to being guarded, but instead being able to keep full dominion over your body and power. When you jump out of your body, no one is home. When you are not home in your body, they can take from you. If you are not home in yourself, people energetically pick that up—unconsciously, of course—and they come in and take from you."

Tej paused and then asked a life-changing question. "Can you feel that even with me, you are not in the lower half of your body?"

Confused, I tried to sense what he meant. I closed my eyes.

"I guess I'm not," I admitted.

"Embodiment is your next piece of work, my dear. Full embodiment."

There was that word again.

"What do you actually mean by embodiment?" I asked with a touch of frustration.

In place of an explanation I was given more questions.

"Can you shift your attention to feel like you are sitting in your heart? Rest back inside the center of your chest. Take a moment to feel that."

I tried to sense the internal space of my body, particularly my chest. "Yes, I guess I can feel that."

"Then, can you be inside your hands?" he asked.

"Yes, I am used to doing that at my Dahn Yoga and Qi Gong class." I felt tingling inside my hands.

"Then notice if you are inside your pelvis or not. Can you sense that?"

I closed my eyes again and tried to feel what he was describing.

"I guess so," I answered, not convinced.

"I don't feel that you are. Can you drop your attention further down into your pelvis, into all your sexual organs?"

I blushed and dropped my attention a little more. I was embarrassed I was doing this in the middle of a normal workday and quickly opened my eyes for a second to make sure the blinds were covering the entire window and no one could see in.

"Let's do a practice here together," he suggested. "Are you open to me becoming more intimate with you? I will stay across the room from you here on this chair. I promise I do not want anything from you, sexually or otherwise. I am very happy and committed in my relationship right now. What I am going to do is give a hundred percent of my attention to you, and I want to see if you can stay in your body."

"Okay," I agreed with some trepidation. Tej always had unconventional ways to give me insights.

I rolled my chair to the side so the desk did not separate us. With every second that passed, he became more and more present and gave me more and more attention. I could feel the intensity of his energy and it was uncomfortable.

"Now I want you to feel the entire internal space of your pelvis while I give even more attention to you."

I dropped my attention further down into my body, and I immediately started to feel my pelvis pulse. I felt the width of my hips. I felt my butt in the chair. His eyes got more loving, intense, and present. Everything in me wanted to jump out of my body, but Tej caught it. "Stay there. I love to see you in this way. I love your feminine essence. I love that you are allowing me to see you."

I was becoming aroused in the chair. My face flushed a brighter pink, but my mind knew it had nothing to do with Tej. I was in contact with myself and my own feminine energy while a strong masculine presence was giving me a lot of attention. The polarity that becomes present when the opposites poles of feminine and masculine come together was alive in my office. I kept breathing and sinking lower and deeper into my pelvis. *This is what is meant by embodiment,* I thought. Time stood still. Fear subsided. My presence grew more alive and awakened, and I felt it easier to hold his gaze.

Tej nodded, and in his soft, tender voice said, "Thank you. That is your practice. Don't ever leave your pelvis, your sexuality, your sensuality around a man again. This power is for you, not him. Don't let him take it."

I stayed quiet, feeling the internal space of my body, down to my feet and through my hands.

"I didn't realize how scared I was of intimacy until right now," I said, embarrassed. "Also, a part of me becomes scared that if I really show my sexuality and passion with a man, I'm going to be too intense for him and he will leave."

Tej's answer was simply, "You are not too much for me, and you will not be too much for the right man for you. "Don't overthink what just happened," he instructed. "Just keep practicing the sensation of resting in your pelvis." He got up and gave me a kiss on the forehead. The door closed behind him and I was left there—somehow changed.

The pulsing throughout my body was rhythmic. I had received his full attention, and I remained embodied in my sexuality. I realized I had never been able to stay grounded in the presence of a masculine man. This felt powerful, like an important piece of my love story. Yet after this expansion settled, like peeling back another layer of an onion, another deeper fear emerged. I was afraid of making love.

I felt sexy most of the time, but I was afraid of sex. I'd had six sexual experiences in my twenties. I was scared that these men would realize I was not as exciting as my sensual facade, and instead they would experience a stilted, unexpressed version of what their fantasy had led them to believe.

Looking back, I don't know when I started shutting down in bed, which I have since learned happens to most women but manifests in different ways.

While growing up, I never saw my mum's cleavage or thighs other than when she was in a swimsuit or getting in and out of the shower. I was aware of her feminine sensuality, even though she kept it covered. I saw it in photos taken in her twenties, and one day I found several negligees in the back of her top bedroom drawer. I pulled out one that was hemmed with lace and stuffed it under my arm when no one was looking. The innocent, romantic 10-year-old me stood in front of the mirror on top of her dresser and felt her sensuality for the first time. The feeling of the cool silk on her flat chest and the lavender scent from the bags Mum always had in her drawers. I imagined how beautiful I would be with my own nightie like this. The next time I knew no one would enter my bedroom unannounced,

I borrowed one of her bras. I hooked it at the front, twisted it into position, and stuffed four tissues into each cup, then walked over to my mirror again. As I ran my tiny hands over the padded curves and imagined those curves were part of me, pride and anticipation blossomed.

The day I didn't live up to my mum's innocent ideal of me, I felt the impact of her disappointment. At age 16 she found my personal secret diary next to my bed when she was tidying up my room in preparation for my Nana's annual visit. I was giving up my bedroom for her. Even back then I loved interior decorating. I had done my best job at an Asian-themed bedroom with Chinese characters on paper stuck to the wall; fake bamboo plants and a black laughing Buddha were set on the carpet in the corner. Mum sat on my single mattress that lay on the floor as she opened the pages that housed my private, immature thoughts. She was disgusted by the sexual imagery that was sprawled across the page.

She walked into my room later that day with my journal in her hand.

"This is filthy," she stated, waving my diary in the air. "What if one of your younger siblings saw this?"

I was just as angry at her but didn't feel I had the right to say so. Why was she reading my diary?

"They wouldn't. They're not allowed in my room."

"Well, I found it, and they could have read it too. It was right next to your bed. You didn't even have the decency to hide it."

"I always hide it."

"Well, this time you did not."

I felt the sensation of shame overtake me—hers and mine. I couldn't look her in the eye for a week.

I never once remember Mum making me feel bad about not having a boyfriend. We didn't talk about my love life after that day. She asked me to throw away the diary immediately. I did throw it away to honor Mum's wishes. I wanted to live up to her ideal. The next diary I bought, I hid in a much better place. I wrapped it inside an old Michael Jackson T-shirt I had outgrown and stuffed it at the back of my fourth dresser drawer.

As I started to clarify what I wanted in a man after my heartaches in Ashland, I knew I wanted a man who was not an average Joe. I wanted someone who could match with me spiritually as well as sexually. I wanted to be met at the highest level possible. I wanted an extraordinary relationship that would inspire others. I could see the vision of what I wanted; I just hadn't found the right person.

● CHAPTER 21 ●

SING

Two years later, I was still searching for love. It didn't worry me that I wasn't married yet, as marriage wasn't on my agenda. I would tell myself I wanted a spiritual partnership ceremony instead of a wedding. I wanted to be with someone for life but didn't subscribe to the idea that marriage was the doorway to happiness and security. What played on my mind was that I had not yet had a real boyfriend. Thirty-one years old and no one had wanted to date me exclusively for more than a few weeks. I'd never been chosen to be someone's committed partner. What was wrong with me?

More than receiving love, I yearned to give it. I was a great catch, I told myself. As the years went by without even an occasional boyfriend, it was hard not to believe that one of my life lessons was to be alone. I studied the Law of Attraction as if my life depended on it. Why had I experienced such an absence of love when I had so much to give? I'd been asking friends, colleagues, psychics, and any workshop facilitators who would talk to me about why I was always single. They each had different words of wisdom to share—but nothing that helped me. The most common advice was, "You have to be okay being single. When you stop looking, he'll show up." This line of reasoning made me want to punch someone. I needed to connect to my own higher guidance again.

I had learned the hard way that if I were to connect with that Divine voice, I had to be in a state of joy, appreciation, or love.

One time I had lost one of my monthly paychecks. As I sat in my office, I sank into a state of appreciating what I saw around me, the friends staring at me from photo frames, and the sky outside the window. I asked, "Where is the envelope with my paycheck?" I heard the words clearly, "It's in the car." I thought, *Great; that was easy.*

At the end of the workday I went out to my mobile rust bucket, which by then showed more rust than paint. It had been a stressful day, my brain was tired, and I was looking forward to a night zoning out in front of a romantic comedy. I looked through the rubble of food wrappers and empty water bottles in the back seat and passenger seat but didn't see the envelope. I never kept my rusty Chevy clean enough to easily find something, but after five minutes of searching I gave up and thought, *Jeez, looks like my guidance was off.*

The next day, I realized again that I needed that check to cover my bills, so I allowed myself to drift into a state of happiness, felt appreciation for what I had, and again the voice as clear as a bell said, "It's in the car." Later that day I had my own version of Groundhog Day as I opened the doors to the back seat hoping to find the envelope with the check. I climbed over to the driver's side to check the door pocket. After 10 minutes of searching I gave up and said to myself, *What the hell? Why does my guidance say it's in the car? It's not in the car!* I had looked in every nook and cranny to no avail.

I decided to wait a few days to ask again, as perhaps my divine guidance was on vacation. I resumed the practice days later. I got myself happy, grateful, and at peace through some visualizations and thinking of those I loved the most. Then I asked the same question again. I knew I'd hear the right answer this time. The voice said—and I perceived a little more attitude this time—"It's in the car!"

"WTF?"

I took a deep breath and massaged my temples. *Why is it telling me the same incorrect thing every time?* Then I thought to ask, "Can you give me a little more guidance on why I can't find it in the damn car?"

With a sense of humor, the voice said, "You can't find it because you need to be in a higher state when you actually go out to the car."

I realized that I had been going out there at the end of each day stressed from the day and irritated when I couldn't find the check right away. I tried again immediately. I skipped out there, feeling joy and gratitude, took in the sight of the huge oak trees lining the street, and breathed in the rosebushes planted at the front of the office building. I stood in front of the car and asked the voice, "Can you tell me where in the car it is?"

It immediately replied, "In the boot."

Apparently, divine guidance can have an Australian accent. I moved aside an old blanket and an old paper grocery bag in the boot and there it was. My envelope, containing my paycheck.

I came to realize that the state we are in matches the things, people, thoughts, and information that come to us. If I was in a low emotional state, the thoughts sounded similar to, *I don't feel good; this is always going to be hard. I'm not any good at this.* If I felt joy and appreciation and excitement, thoughts like, *I can do this; it's just a matter of time. This will be easier than I thought* would come flooding in. My negativity was preventing me from receiving powerful, accurate guidance.

Sometimes messages came to me through that voice and sometimes visually. One Sunday morning after my usual tea ritual in bed, I was leaning back on a few pillows against the head of my bed when I had the thought, *My ideal man needs to be someone I want to be around a lot.* It's one thing to be attracted to each other for the first six months and another thing to move in together and live in close quarters with each other for 40–50 or more years. I asked the questions: what is my life partner like? Who is the man who will feel so comfortable and right in my home? My eyes were drawn to the bedroom window, and outside I saw a man in the garden. He was working on something. I couldn't make out exactly what. He caught my eye and came toward me with a huge smile. He pressed his nose right up to the window, crossed his eyes, and made the goofiest face. I laughed. *Oh! That's right; I want someone goofy.* I want someone to keep me light and laughing.

One night I decided to have a meeting with this voice about the biggest issue plaguing my otherwise blessed life. I planned to stay in a high vibrational state for this reconnection. I picked up my journal and turned to the next blank page available. I dog-eared the corner and wrote at the top this question: What is the next step I need to take to find my soul mate?

I placed the journal on the side table faceup so I could see the embossed gold letters on the front cover that simply said DREAM. I shuffled into the modest bathroom of the small cottage I now lived in on my own and started to draw a bath laced with lavender oil and epsom salts. The hot bath wound me down into receptivity, followed by some meditation as I sat up in bed. I thought about all the things that I was grateful for, all the people I loved, and how blessed I was. That was easy. I thought of my family, my opportunity to live in the States, and my friends who were so supportive of me. To seal the deal, I looked down and giggled upon seeing my new dog snoring on her blanket. I had gone to the animal shelter the week after my visa was approved because I didn't want to live without the joy of a dog one week longer. I went expecting to bring home a Maltese terrier or Chihuahua, given I'd always had small dogs. Instead I came home with an 85-pound Rottweiler named Hannah. As the energy around me started to feel more expanded and spacious, I opened my journal and copied down the question again: What is the next step that I need to take in order to find my soul mate?

I closed my eyes and rested in the darkness. Just like a picture on a screen coming into focus, something was trying to come into focus behind my eyelids. I waited in gratitude. What appeared was a vision of the black night sky with millions of stars sparkling in the distance. I waited in curiosity. All of a sudden some letters slowly came into focus in the foreground of that black starry night. They became clearer and clearer until I could see the word SING. The word was in capital letters. Then each letter turned into neon colors, and then fireworks started going off in all directions around this word. SING.

No! I didn't want this to be the answer. I resisted the neon sign. *No, no, no!* My last gig in Australia sent me spiraling into depression. It was not my life's calling anymore, and I didn't want to go back to entertaining people just for entertainment's sake. I had received the same so-called insight before: if I sang, it would put me in front of him somehow, he'd be able to find me easier. Now the message was undeniable. I resisted because even though four years earlier I had showed up in America with one suitcase and a guitar, I didn't want to go back to the music industry that had burned me out. That time in my life had passed. Spirituality and personal development were my main loves now. Nevertheless, it said SING. In capitals. With fireworks.

I'd prefer to forget about the last full singing performance in Australia because of my fragile ego. The type of music I mostly got paid for in Australia was covers. I sang at weddings, parties, nightclubs, bars, airports, on the street, festivals, schools, football stadiums, and wherever else they would pay me. Sometimes no one would listen because they were too busy talking with their friends, sometimes people would dance, sometimes we felt like rock stars and were asked for autographs, and sometimes I had to be security guard for the band—pushing drunk people back after they crashed into our microphones. *It has to be easier than this,* I would often think, while singing "I Will Survive" at the top of my lungs.

I had studied jazz and popular music performance and business at college and loved being a student because I could really let my creativity flow. Eventually, I started to write my own music. I recorded my debut CD *City Girls* in 1999. It was a great learning experience, as I worked with the best of the best musicians in Melbourne (which is home to many of the best musicians in the world). We had an amazing CD launch at the Prince Patrick Hotel. It was the quintessential Aussie pub—dirty hardwood floors, huge bar, high ceilings, grungy atmosphere packed with lots of alternative cool-looking people. This night we had a full house and an eight-piece band behind me. I was blinded by the stage lights, but I was in heaven.

I did a few gigs with the larger band and my original music with a few covers thrown in there, but it was too hard to pay so many musicians and still have anything left at the end of the night unless I could pack the house every time. That was a lot of marketing pressure I didn't want. I had a full-time business teaching singing at various high schools, colleges, and from my home studio. I didn't know how to market and sell myself well or find the time for it. I had the idea that to move my original music forward I needed do gigs with another person, ideally a guitarist who could sing well enough to do backing harmonies, who also had followers so they could attract some people to the gigs as well. This was a leap outside my comfort zone because I wasn't particularly great at playing guitar. Without a band to cover that up, I felt more exposed.

I found the right person, the masterful singer-songwriter folk guitar player Paul Wookey. I was nervous about the first gig we had. I wanted it to be special. I wanted to blow everyone away, as we had at my first CD launch. Just so you know, I'm a perfectionist. I wanted it to be perfect, first time out of the gate. I had visions of a hundred tea light candles, a dimly lit room, and impressing the pants off everyone. Instead, my guitar playing was average. We hadn't rehearsed enough. Paul's songs were better than mine. What I remembered the day after the gig was that it was an okay performance, but nowhere near exceptional. The way it probably was in the audience's mind was a good night out. I wanted spectacular. I wanted extraordinary. I wanted to have them be talking about that night for weeks. I didn't get the result I wanted. I didn't want to do another one. I told Paul I needed to regroup and think about it. I felt my confidence shaken to the core. Because of my crazy internal standards that often kept me imprisoned, I would end up not doing another live gig for five years.

CHAPTER 22

KARAOKE DOWN UNDER

A few weeks after I received the message to SING, Tej and I traveled to Sydney to lead a training for the Foundation. I still didn't have the guts to quit and go off on my own, even though my desire for that was growing by the week. The neon sign, however, that had appeared in my mind was still causing me mental anguish.

The word SING scared me because I didn't know if my soul's purpose was to return to being a singer. I didn't want that. *Would my Higher Power force me to do something I didn't want to do?* I didn't want to start singing again. I was done with that, I would say to myself. Yet another voice would say, *Maybe I should sing because I know it's a gift I have, so why throw it away?*

I told Tej I was considering singing again. He didn't even know whether I could hold a tune. He did his best to help me process through the blocks that arose without knowing my history, but within days, divine timing stepped in. One of the retreat participants raised their voice to declare, "We're going out to a karaoke night." Others smiled at the idea of the silliness and fun of that. Tej looked at me and responded, "We're coming with you."

I changed into something sassier, layered on more makeup, and caught a taxi with Tej and the group of eight that had formed for a night on the town. We hopped out onto downtown's busiest nightclub street and through a narrow door and dark, dingy passageway. We were shown the way to our private karaoke room by a cute Japanese girl in her late teens. "Someone will be wiv you soon to give you instruction," she said with a thick accent.

Our room was pitch-black except for the light near the electronics station where you could choose your song and a few points of light on the walls, creating a bad impersonation of the night sky. I hadn't sung in front of anyone for five years. I sat on a bench built into the wall and joined in the giggles as everyone chose a song and did their best with it.

My turn came in the karaoke lineup. None of the group knew I had sung professionally. None of them had ever heard me even humming a tune, let alone sing "Hot Stuff" by Donna Summer at full force, which I did that night. When I was done, I casually gave the next person the microphone and noticed everyone's jaws hanging open. The sound through the speakers was perfect. It was cued to make anyone sound great. I felt the powerful embodied feeling that I used to get when I sang, and then I casually sat down.

"What the hell?" someone said.

From the darkness another voice said, "Why are you not singing?"

"You're incredible."

"You're more than incredible," Tej said.

The shock and joy on their faces motivated me to punch more song requests into the computer. Carole King. Olivia Newton-John. The Eagles. With each time up to the microphone I was reminded of a skill I had mastered and a beloved feeling that danced with me when I sang for fun. Everyone had a great time, and eventually some of them talked about leaving for the night. I wasn't ready to go home. A cork had been popped.

The cute Japanese girl had to kick me out at midnight. My friends had to pull my shoulder as I was trying to punch in another song request. I eventually made my way back out onto the bustling street of neon lights and billboards. My elation turned to tears around one o'clock, when in the silence of my own company I realized just how much I had missed that feeling. The grief that showed itself to me after five years without a performance rocked me to sleep.

The next day, Tej asked me to sing a song for the group.

"No, I don't think that is appropriate." I didn't want to take time from our process work.

"They will love it, are you kidding?" he said when he realized how much my heels were dug in about not wanting to sing again. "Let's just see how it feels and how they react."

I budged and said okay. With relief I realized I needed a guitar, so I told them why I couldn't sing.

"I have one; I can bring it tomorrow," announced one of the participants.

Damn. "Okay, I'll perform a song tomorrow."

In the middle of the tug-of-war inside me I realized that if I didn't have any expectations for myself, I loved to sing. When expectations were present, I felt stifled. For some reason I felt I would be wasting people's time because their growth process was more important than being entertained.

The next morning, I cut my fingernails at the basin, warmed up with some scales in the front of the mirror, and felt nauseous. In front of the eager circle I picked up the sunburst acoustic guitar, closed my eyes, and sang the type of song I liked most to sing— alternating between softness and belting.

I let the final ring of the guitar strings settle and opened my eyes. Some of the women were sniffling, some looked like they were meditating, and Tej was gently nodding his head.

Grief, relief, and inspiration intertwined themselves around my heart and the decision was made.

When I arrived back in Ashland from that trip, I decided to start a band. I didn't want to put much time and effort into it, as I didn't know where this would end up. I'd only do this if opportunities opened easily. In days I heard from an artist friend of mine that a music and art festival was coming up, and it accepted 20–25 musical acts each year to play on the grounds of the old Briscoe School.

Maybe I could get a few people to back me and I could sing some of my original songs and some covers, I thought. The only person I knew personally who played an instrument at the professional level I was accustomed to was Datta from Toast-masters. I had seen him play a few high-level gigs, and we'd played in the infamous Toastmaster band that got together annually for our Christmas party and attempted to stay in time and in tune while having a blast over whiskey, wine, and too much food.

After Toastmasters one night I approached my friend. "Do you have a moment, Datta? I want to ask you about something."

"Sure."

I walked him to the corner of the room, beside the Toast-masters official banner and American flag, as if I had a secret that I didn't want anyone else to hear.

"Do you want to play in my band for the Briscoe festival? I'm thinking of pulling a quartet together, just drums, bass, and electric guitar, and I can sing and play acoustic guitar. Would you be my bass player?"

Without hesitation he said yes. We'd been friends for three years at Toastmasters, so I felt a level of comfort with him as I shared my vision for the band and type of repertoire I wanted to do.

"That sounds perfect," he said. "How about we meet for tea this week to talk about who we could ask to play with us and to hear more about what you have in mind."

"Great idea." *Could things fall into place this easily?* I thought. I was feeling led again. Doors were opening for this, but I could still feel I had the hand brake only half released. What I didn't know until much later is that the previous year Datta had also come to the conclusion that he didn't just want to entertain people. He wanted to inspire and enlighten. Months before I asked him to be my bass player, he quit four of the bands he played with and decided he was done with entertaining for its own sake. "But," he told his friends, "if Rachael Jayne ever asked me to be in her band, I'd say yes in a heartbeat."

We met for tea at my favorite spot—the café on top of Bloomsbury Bookstore. Datta was well connected with other top-level musicians in town and had played with most of them. I liked Datta as a person—a lot. He was an excellent speaker and made me laugh every time we interacted. But I had a lot of random judgments about him that made me think we'd never be best buddies. My friend Beril had tried to set me up with him many times, thinking we'd be perfect for each other. "Do you get that Datta is the catch of the town?" she had asked me on many occasions. She thought I might have been interested romantically, so she checked in first with my intentions. As soon as I assured her I was not, she proceeded to set him up with her single girlfriends.

Datta was not what all women would call the "catch of the town." He was a little on the eccentric and goofy side. But he was Beril and her husband's salsa dance instructor, her speech coach, and her friend, so she saw aspects of him that I didn't.

I thought he had too much drama going on in his life, apparently getting over a difficult relationship. I judged him for wearing a beret that wasn't in style and for wearing T-shirts that had been left in the dryer too long—he would often give the audience a glimpse of his tummy when he'd raise his arms during one of his animated speeches. He put himself one hundred percent into everything he did. I knew he was a sincere, generous, smart, and hilarious guy, just not the Tom Selleck type—tall, dark, and mysterious—that I still told myself I wanted.

Without the need to impress or flirt, I relaxed over jasmine green tea and found myself telling him about the vulnerable moment I had after singing those karaoke tunes Down Under. As I shared the moment with him, I was transported back in time to the karaoke room in Sydney. The Japanese girl, the faces of my friends, and the feeling of not wanting to leave at midnight. I was talking so fast about what happened, so caught up in it that I forgot he was there for a moment. I finally looked over the table at him, and his focus on me brought me right back to the present.

"Does that sound stupid?" I asked. "Is it stupid that I want to start singing again?"

His response was like a warm, gentle hug. "No, it's not stupid. Your story is beautiful." He had the kindest eyes, and I could feel how much he was on my side. We now shared a vision for the band.

We found two more members without a struggle—a drummer and a lead guitarist. Datta suggested we rehearse at his house because he had an excellent sound system. We all had fun together. The band started to sound good. Datta and I would hang out after the others went home, sip tea, and talk. He started to call me on the phone at random times to talk about different things. I liked that. We became confidantes. Beril still was trying to encourage me to take it a step further, but I was clear we were just friends.

Then, just like in the movies, one look changed everything. I don't know which rehearsal it was, but I looked over at him playing his fire-engine-red bass and he looked back at me, and in an instant something sparked between us. The veil of my judgments parted, and I saw a handsome, powerful, smart, and sexy guy who had been supporting me in this endeavor for the last few months and wasn't asking for anything in return. After that rehearsal, while we had our usual tea time at his kitchen table, I noticed I wanted to be physically closer to him. I found my bare feet wanting to touch his. At the same time my head was saying, *What are you thinking? It's Datta from Toastmasters.* I moved my foot closer and let it almost touch. I did not have the guts for that bold move.

All the bands that wanted to perform at Briscoe had to send an audition tape or CD. Only a few headliners were paid, and the rest were happy to play for the exposure. We were among those happy for the exposure, but when the decision came, we were surprised to be picked as a paid headliner.

Our performance at the festival that clear June day was a hit. We were the new band on the scene, with a packed audience on the grassy hill in front of our stage under a massive elm tree. I was flirtatious with the audience—and with my bass player. I was filled with innocence. Many of my friends that day affirmed that taking up singing again was a great idea for me. A few asked, "What's going on with you and Datta?"

"Nothing," I replied.

CHAPTER 23

LOVE AT FIRST SIGHT IS A MYTH

What I would call my first date with Datta happened on a Monday night. He created art over his stove as I watched from his modest birch dining table. There is something very sexy about a man who knows how to cook. Delicious smells wafted past me as I took in his home like I hadn't before.

Clearly, no woman lived there. Plants were his form of decoration, and he put function before form. The chair where I sat didn't match the table. The TV cabinet didn't match the accent table next to it, and the gold stretchy sofa cover hid an old couch that was in desperate need of some throw pillows. I realized I was judging him and reminded myself, *I'm not looking for a throw-pillow kind of guy.*

I'd gone away for the weekend on a training I had led for the Foundation, and we both wanted to watch the movie *The Secret* to see what all the fuss was about, so Monday night it was. As he served up Indian food, I learned he'd studied with top vegetarian chefs on every continent. He didn't yet know I was a quadruple Taurus and that food was the speediest way to my heart. I was falling fast with every perfectly spiced mouthful.

Datta was smooth. If I had known how much of a romancer he was in our earlier years at Toastmasters, I would have fallen right away. He had shown romantic interest in me ten days prior. At least I interpreted it as romantic. Before that Monday night date, he'd read me his poetry, he fed me magic beans (my pet name for cocoa-covered almonds that he would bring over for after our band rehearsals), and he gave me plenty of long hugs and some lingering looks with those deep-set, intense ocean-blue eyes.

He put *The Secret* into the DVD player and sat back on the couch next to me. After only a quarter of the movie he reached out his hand, palm up, inviting me to take it. I took it. He nuzzled my head. My eyebrow lifted. I didn't know what he was doing. Was there something in my hair? I didn't care, though. It felt good. His nose got closer to mine with each passing interview on Law of Attraction until our eyes met. His kiss fell in line with the way I loved to be kissed. My body melted into his. His presence was palpable, and time slowed down. Senses heightened. Our first magical kiss lasted nearly an hour until we heard Neale's voice emanating from the TV screen. With our bodies interlocked we laughed hysterically. My boss had a scene in the movie, but it didn't stop our momentum. We went back to making out and talking intimately for another hour. Time passed as we talked about the last few weeks together. We joked about who would play us if ever a movie was made about us. Bruce Willis was definitely his counterpart, with his bald head and goatee. He told me I was definitely more Jennifer Aniston than Angelina Jolie. I confessed I hadn't seen this romance coming and wasn't attracted until quite recently.

Datta, in his cheeky bad-boy way, replied, "If I had wanted to date you, you would have known about it and you would've had no choice but to fall hard, baby." I giggled, believing he was probably telling the truth.

He stroked my hair, sending chills down my spine. "You know, you're the perfect woman for me," he said. "I'm amazed I didn't see it sooner. But hey," he continued, "better to be late to the party than miss it altogether."

As soon as the words left his mouth, I felt a warm glow over my entire body. "You probably tell that to all the girls."

"No way!" He shook his head and smiled mischievously. "Maybe there's a way I can prove it to you," he announced as he stood up and left the room.

He brought back a handwritten list that took up three pieces of paper, folded in thirds. On it included all the qualities he had written down within the last year, describing in detail what he wanted to manifest in a romantic life partner. He asked me if I wanted him to share it.

My initial thought was, *I didn't know that guys made lists. At least not more than one or two items.* I wanted to know what was on his list.

With the innocence of a six-year-old boy and the sexiness of an experienced man, he read his list. I was everything on that list. He was confident. He had reason to be. He sent me home that night with shaky knees, and a chant that kept escaping my mouth: "Oh my ... Oh my ... Oh my."

Our second date occurred the following night. We went to an Italian restaurant in town that happened to be a favorite of both of ours, followed by dancing at a local dance space that Datta loved. He was a dancer. Salsa, tango, free-form dance—he was up for practically anything. There was no awkwardness carried into the evening from the previous night, just excitement and disbelief that this was happening with Datta from Toastmasters. It felt so right, but I was acutely aware that I had been in this situation before. I knew it could be taken away from me at any time.

On the third day he called me at noon. I was driving to pick up lunch from the deli and immediately recognized his anxiousness. "There's something I need to tell you before we go any further. It could possibly be a deal breaker for you. Can we meet tonight to talk?"

His seriousness and the lack of clues about what this could be made my heart and stomach both clench. I could see history playing out once again. *It's over before it begins. What could be so bad that would stop this train of love?* I thought. *What could be so wrong that would stop this feeling of everything being so right?*

My mind came up with worst-case scenarios all afternoon long. *He's still married and he hasn't told me. If he was separated, I could handle that. He was sent to prison for seriously injuring someone years ago. I could possibly handle that, if there was a good reason. Maybe he was imprisoned for molesting a child. Oh my, I don't think I could ever be okay with that. That's it! He's a child molester. Oh, my God. It's over before it begins—again.*

I was terrified to hear the news he was going to deliver. He knocked on my door that night with a solemn face. I fixed some tea and we went out to my back deck that warm late June evening. "I'm sorry to have to bring this up and make you feel uncomfortable, but if this relationship is to work in the way I think it can, I need to start with complete honesty. I have something to share that could be a deal breaker for you. Are you okay if I start?"

I nodded. I braced again for the words to hit me.

"I have judgments about arrogant people," he said and paused. I waited for him to continue. He didn't continue.

"What?"

"I have judgments about arrogant people," he repeated, deadpan.

"That was the thing you wanted to tell me?"

"Yes," he replied, waiting for my answer.

"You're not serious?"

He was. "It's been with me all my life. There was a lot of that in my extended family, and it's something I haven't fully reconciled."

"That's really it?" I asked, confused. "You don't like arrogant people?"

He sighed. "It's not that I don't like them. I have friends who are arrogant." He shrugged. "It's just that I give them lots of space. Lots and lots of space."

I didn't mean to, but I couldn't hold my laughter back. "That's it? That's what you thought might be a deal breaker for me?"

He nodded, not super happy I couldn't stop laughing.

"I don't mind if you judge arrogant people. I judge people who pretend to be humble. We'll cancel each other out." I cracked up again.

Our romance continued. Days turned into weeks. I had never had a real relationship hit the four-week mark. We laughed and celebrated that milestone as if I had won a gold medal at the Olympics.

I had been wrong about Datta in many ways. I have never been so wrong about anything or anyone in my life. I was so wrong about the thing that mattered most to me in my life— love. I was wrong about who would be capable of loving me. I had put him in the category of "not my type"—for three freaking years. All those years he'd been right in front of my nose at Toastmasters. He was so right—I mean, so unbelievably, sexily, passionately, beautifully right. He was right for my body, my heart, my mind—and my soul.

I wasn't the only one to blame. He had his judgments about me. I was too young and immature for him, and for some reason he thought I wanted to return to Australia. The few times he had seen Neale speak, he was left with the impression that he was arrogant and a fraud. He assumed I was one of his groupies, and whenever he found himself attracted to me, he derailed that train because he didn't know how it would work, having to tell me what he thought about my boss.

Love at first sight as a romantic ideal is a terrible myth. Datta and I are living proof of that. We were in front of each other for three years. People tend to judge each other too fast—which is exactly what we did. Even though we were both good readers of energy and people, those judgments about each other kept us from thinking of each other as potential soul mates.

I'm not sure when I put two and two together. The inner voice had told me to go to Toastmasters to meet my guy and then it created a neon sign to sing. Datta and I fell deeply in love. I felt invincible because of the connection we instantly had and the accurate connection and answers I was getting from the Divine. It had been leading me all the way—into the arms of love.

Datta struck me as honest. His strongest values were truth-telling, integrity, and owning mistakes. I saw him full of compassion. Datta was a strong, solid, protective guy with the softest of underbellies. His intense love for his family, especially his two sons, was attractive. They were just like him: talented, affectionate, spiritually centered, handsome, and untamable. We loved that we were both vegetarian, and mealtimes were always an intimate experience for us. We fed each other from each other's fork or spoon—every single meal we were together.

We were oblivious to everyone else around us as we enjoyed our feeding ritual. We took time to savor each other in all ways. He inspired me to attain my full feminine essence. I'd finally found someone as romantic as me. His spiritual path was of greatest importance to him, and to top it off he had the best sense of humor of anyone I'd ever met. He had me laughing for the first 30 days of our relationship. On day 31, however, the laughter stopped.

CHAPTER 24

THE POWER OF ANGER

I admitted to Datta on our first date that I was on the brink of leaving the Foundation for my own dream. He was in full support, but I still had a compelling reason to hold off. Would my future business income match my current steady paycheck? The numbers on that check had increased, but I was still living month-to-month with a new car payment, higher rent, and more expensive tastes in clothes.

I had advertised my own coaching business multiple times in the past but only attracted one client for a whopping $350 per month. Patty's reaction to my future career dream made me doubt myself even more. With a perfect balance of trying to help me and trying to put me in my place, she said, "The reason why Neale is successful at this business is because he's well known, and people want to come to his programs and retreats. You would not be selling the programs you are now if it wasn't for Neale."

Her words became the chorus of a bad song repeating itself in my mind. I kept working for the Foundation month after month, year after year. I grew less energized and more bored. My back was also starting to bother me, which hadn't happened in 10 years.

I was not in the flow of life anymore. That was clear. I resisted where the current wanted to take me. My body told me loud and clear. It hurt to sit for more than an hour at a time. I was tired. It was quick to get angry at things that I could have laughed off. I didn't want to be of service to someone else's dream anymore. I wanted my own dream. I wanted my own retreats. I wanted my own best-selling book.

Back in 2004, *feminine energy* and *feminine essence* were new phrases to the circles I moved in. I understood that the feminine principle needed to be more honored in our communities and within ourselves, so the title "The YIN Project" came to me and my little side business was born. Since its conception, I have filled an entire journal of ideas that I could teach and descriptions about the tribe of women I wanted to serve. I received plentiful insights into my own feminine energy and how I had disconnected from my feminine essence, and that was part of why I had not attracted the romantic relationship I wanted into my life. That led me to think about how many of my other friends were in the same boat.

One of them was Marion. She had been the first person to sign up for the CWG Leadership Program. I remember the day I picked up the phone and heard her share how excited she was to do the program. I felt terrible about how quickly I judged her gravelly smoker's voice and the overly confident way she spoke. I felt her roughness and buried anger issues and had some concern having her in the program, but I wanted my first sale. She was in.

When I met her in person, I thought, *She looks how she sounds—weathered by life and determined.* She was already a CWG fan, and after completing the program and being hired on staff, she became my biggest fan. She was boisterous, harsh, and had a foul mouth, but was smart, ambitious, and supported me all the way.

"I recognize talent when I see it. The Foundation would be fucked if it wasn't for you," she announced in the quietest voice I'd heard come from her.

She had invited herself into my office to share some ideas for growth of the Leadership program and didn't want anyone to hear the first of many private conversations we shared.

"Do you want to come over to my place for dinner this week? I'd love for you to meet my kids, and we can talk more about these ideas."

"Sure. How about Thursday?"

Every Thursday night became our ritual of Chinese takeout and hours of discussion and pontification in the living room of her apartment. While the inner circle were soaking in the hot tub or playing board games at Neale's, we were cooking up ways we could grow the Foundation and finally earn the salary we deserved. We felt like a team. I'd never made more than $36,000 a year. That was the highest they had ever paid anyone, even the executive director.

"You deserve to be paid at least twice what you are now," she said. "I know how to help you do it."

She became my closest girlfriend.

She also proved to be a powerful influence. She helped me go to bat for a $20,000-a-year increase and we won. Was this a sign I should stay working for them for a while longer, or was this a test?

How was I going to tell Marion after all the time she had put in to help me win the raise that I felt my soul calling was to leave and start The YIN Project? I let the news slip one night over sweet and sour soup. "I'm not going to be of service to anyone else's dream or mission. I want my own."

I pulled out my journal and shared some highlights of my vision for The YIN Project. She loved it.

Within a week she had outlined how we should go into business together.

Whoa, too fast, I thought, but I didn't have the guts to tell her. I could always feel a strong undertone of "Don't fuck with me" even though I knew she loved me. She talked about the weaker links at the Foundation in a crass tone when they weren't in the room, and a part of me thought it mightn't take much to get on the wrong side of her. Still, her selfless, protective, generous side was always on display when it came to me, and that is what bonded our friendship.

She saw me as a golden goose. She would use those exact words. She wanted a part of that. She also brought a lot of business acumen I didn't have to the table. I never clearly agreed or disagreed about being official business partners. I just kept dodging the conversation and we kept dreaming together.

As more people rubbed up against her personality, they didn't trust her. I didn't know if I could either, but I wanted to. She was my biggest supporter.

Our plan to escape the Foundation solidified in a Word document on both our computers. We had the revenue model, the things we could sell, but didn't know where we were going to find prospects. Ashland was a town of 20,000 people and was saturated with spiritual training.

I admitted to Marion, "I know we have to take this online, but I am still so scared of what will happen if it's not successful."

Every time she looked at me, I could feel how much she believed in me. "Let me show you why you have to do this. Why we have to do this." She pulled out a piece of paper from her printer drawer and drew a line down the middle with a Sharpie. At the top right-hand side of the page she wrote "Reasons to Stay" and on the left side, "Reasons to Go."

"There's only one reason to stay," I declared.

I placed her coffee table book of the Oregon mountains under the paper and wrote in big letters: SECURE PAYCHECK.

I thought I could list many reasons to leave on the other side of the paper, but I found myself closing my eyes and receiving the only reason that really mattered. I wrote in bigger letters: TO FOLLOW MY SOUL'S CALLING.

In what would be my last retreat with Neale, I sat in the back of the hall and was triggered by almost everything he said from his Guru chair. I blamed him for not being more evolved and honest. I blamed him for not entertaining me anymore. I blamed him for saying the same story the same way, every single bloody time. I started to overheat when others would laugh at his 10-year-old jokes.

Master Young Hee had continued to be a source of support for Neale and a mentor to me. She approached me on the final night of the retreat to find out why I seemed so angry. Like never before I unloaded a monologue of anger and frustration as political correctness sprinted out the door.

"How can you stand it? How can you listen to this word for word every time time? How can you reconcile that the man is not the message? How are you okay giving up your life to support his?"

I was not the type to have anger issues, nor did I talk to my seniors like that, but I was fuming. She let me rage on without stopping me.

"How can you accept him being one person onstage and someone else offstage? It's boring!"

After I had finished my tirade, she simply looked at me with her sweet Korean smile and gently blew air out of her mouth.

"Why are you smiling at me?" I snapped.

She said, "Congratulations. This is a wonderful day for you."

"What do you mean?"

"You don't need Daddy anymore. You are ready to take your own stage. You shouldn't be angry; you should be celebrating."

"What?"

Young Hee took a deep breath and again gently blew it across her lips as if she were exhaling my resistance. Her unconditional love turned the fire in my eyes to water.

"Your being angry at Neale has nothing to do with him. Isn't it time to let this anger fuel your larger desire?" she asked. "And just so you know," she inserted as she stood up to leave, "I don't feel like I am giving up my life for Neale or anyone. I am living my soul's purpose right here and right now. I am happily in service for myself just as much as for him. You, my dear, are not."

Like the Karate Kid with Mr. Miyagi, I had to unravel and piece together what she was telling me. It was time to move on. I had outgrown the operation. I was the only one to blame for my frustration. I was projecting my anger at myself onto Young Hee and Neale because I chose to stay. All the desires within me that had been pushed down for so long escaped to the surface at that retreat.

I learned that one of the reasons we become angry is that we ignore our desires or allow someone else to ignore our desires. Anger was the energy I needed to feel the potency of my desire. My soul now wanted to be in service to my own mission. I just needed to put belief in myself together with my game plan and find a way to make money to stay in the country—preferably as a legal alien.

I wasn't being seen, first by myself. I wasn't on the road I wanted. I'd veered off my soul's road at least a year prior, and I wasn't making quick enough turns to get back on the right path and pick up the next Divine Breadcrumb. I just kept driving off the road out of fear. I was bound to crash into something soon.

• CHAPTER 25 •

STRANDED IN LONDON

I admit I wore too high of a heel most days to try to disguise the weight I had put on since adopting a more American carb- and sugar-filled diet. Sitting in front of a computer all day only made my back pain worse. I would stretch my glutes and hamstrings out on the floor of my office, but exercise didn't seem to help much. I didn't want to sit anymore. I wanted to stand—on a stage.

One of the greatest perks of my job was travel, as I was usually the one sent with Neale to organize the training, but on Day 30 of the intensifying relationship with Datta, I was not in the mood to go. After a long overnight flight, I arrived at Heathrow with an overweight suitcase rolling beside me and a computer bag over my shoulder.

I adopted a shoestring budget approach because I worked for a non-profit. That's why, when I arrived a few days before the training began to recover from my jetlag, I decided to stay with Sarah, one of the participants in the program, who felt like a soul sister. I took the train versus a taxi across London from the airport, and I found myself stuck at the bottom of one of those never-ending flights of stairs at the lower floor of London's Tube. No beam of light shone down from street level. No elevator was in sight, and everyone was rushing too quickly to get anyone's attention. I decided that even though my back was sore, I did not want to embarrass myself by stopping someone and asking for help to carry one side of my suitcase up the stairs with me. So as any independent woman would do, I lugged my 60-pound suitcase and computer bag up two flights of stairs on my own. If I had only known that a split-second decision could have such a devastating impact for years to come, I would have begged every last person in that stairwell.

By dinner I was in serious trouble. I had a hard time sitting on Sarah's chic wooden bench at her dining table. "My back is very sore after the long trip. I think I'm going to bow out early tonight," I apologized.

"I understand. Do you think a bath would help to relax your muscles?" she asked, seeing my discomfort.

"It couldn't hurt, I guess."

I guessed wrong. I had forgotten everything I knew about inflamed spinal discs. They loved ice. Instead, I slipped into the hottest bath I could stand.

In the middle of the night I woke up in Sarah's flat in the most excruciating pain I'd ever experienced. I couldn't move without yelping like an injured dog. If I moved even an inch, pain would surge up and down my body, bringing me close to losing consciousness. I couldn't even bear the slight movement of the mattress as I breathed. I pulled myself off the mattress, thankfully lying on the floor, and slithered inch by inch like a snake until I reached the hardwood floor in the living room. I waited there with tears rolling down my cheeks until Sarah awoke.

I called Datta from Sarah's living room floor, sobbing into the speakerphone she had positioned next to my chin. I explained what happened, trying to not move. "I don't know what to do. I'm in so much pain."

"Oh, sweetie, I wish I was there. I feel helpless here. I hate that."

I held back my response. Any time I spoke, it sent shock waves down my limp legs.

"It's going to be okay, Beautiful. Can Sarah help you get to the emergency room?"

The care in his voice released more tears down my face. I couldn't reach to wipe them away.

I had no idea what to do. I didn't know what was worse, the physical torture or the emotional plummet, fearing that it could be weeks if not months before I was able to sit long enough to fly home to see my new love. I thought, *Men don't hang around for long.* What was going to make Datta want to commit to a cripple?

We spent two hours figuring out a way to raise me up off the floor and then another four hours to transport me to a hospital. I didn't want to call an ambulance in a foreign country for fear of the cost. After an agonizing day and strong medication, I could walk a few steps, albeit slowly and leaning severely to my right. My left side was the culprit. Three herniated discs pushed on every nerve within range. I could stand with support, and I could lie on my stomach with a specific arch in my back, but that was it. I couldn't sit or lie on my back or get into any comfortable state even with the strongest of painkillers.

A few days later, Sarah shipped my luggage ahead and I somehow put myself on a train and stood holding myself up by the handlebars for hours, all the way up north to Newcastle Upon Tyne, where my best friend from high school, Fiona, lived. She was now an osteopath and ran her own clinic. She looked after me for two months in her home while I became well enough to endure the two long plane flights from England to Oregon.

Back in Australia, Mum and Dad were deeply concerned. He'd had a bad back all his life, so they knew that challenge intimately. Back in Oregon, Datta was showing signs that he might see me through this disaster. He did what he could to cheer me up. He called every day and would read poetry that he had written for me. Being in love was the best painkiller I'd ever been offered. Our relationship, at least for now, had to be long-distance. He wanted to fly over to England and help me come back home, but neither of us had the money. We would have needed an international round trip ticket for him and a first-class lie-down bed for me because I couldn't sit. Such a plan would cost $8,000.

That day in the London Tube started a two-year journey of not being able to walk properly, sit for any length of time, or sleep for more than two hours at a stretch. I was always sleep-deprived, in pain, and drugged with Vicodin and Percocet. I prayed for time to speed up while the drugs kicked in to save my sanity. I lived a physical hell. The shame was almost as bad. Many people in town knew me as someone who traveled the world and taught people how they create their own reality. I could feel them pondering behind my back—and sometimes out loud—*Why did she create this for herself?*

Many reasons were advanced, and I think they are all true to a certain degree. Some thought this was self-sabotage after starting my relationship with Datta. Some thought it was a karmic lineage that I was carrying on for my family, as almost all of us had back issues.

I grew sick of people telling me not only the reasons for my difficulty, but the latest thing that cured their sister, mother, son, or friend from their back injury. Some of them—including doctors—told me surgery was the only option. Everyone knew what had worked for a different person's body, but I needed to know what my body was telling me. I found a gifted healer and world-class kinesiologist, Gary Ferguson, who'd cured himself of terminal brain cancer after being given months to live while traveling internationally as a world-class trumpet player and a principal in the Boston Symphony. One of his first remarks was that the ground I was living on was literally not supporting my back.

I knew this was true because I had already received guidance to move from Ashland, where everybody pretty much thought the same way. One example of that was seeing only one John McCain sign in Ashland during the 2008 election. When Obama won, thousands flocked to the city plaza to celebrate. I was shocked by the levity and dancing on the streets. Aussies only celebrated like that if they won the World Cup. Politics Down Under were anything but exciting. I wanted to experience more diversity, especially diversity of thought. I had no room to expand in Ashland. Gary said I needed to step more into my own domain of being a spiritual teacher—and I wasn't doing that.

All these reasons may have had some degree of validity, but when I look back now, I realize the primary reason was that I was not in the flow of my life. As long as I live, I never want to forget that. I'd veered off my soul's path. I was not pointed in the direction of my divine longing. I was not in flow with the guidance I'd received and had tried to override it. I attempted to keep my boat in the same place along the river as the strong current tried to take me downstream. For over two years the knowing voice inside me had urged me to find a way to leave the Foundation and start my own training.

At some level I had to create an event that would kick me out of the nest of the Foundation and into following my own dream. I hesitated to jump off the cliff because I knew I'd probably crash into rocks below. Sometimes I feared I would never recover from imminent failure, so I kept choosing the comfort of what I knew. As my intention to leave became stronger, something had to give. I remember Nancy Walsch, Neale's ex-wife, saying to add this statement after setting an intention: "Let my intention come in an easy and non-painful way."

On a conscious level I realized that creating my back injury was the most efficient way to stop me working for the Foundation. On an unconscious level—a factor I was completely unaware of at the time—this injury created a way for me to stop growing. I had a deep unconscious fear that if I kept growing—personally and spiritually—I would outgrow my man. I was now unable to move, sit, or meditate. I'd never had a man who fully met me and was compatible on all levels. I was now experiencing that and didn't want to lose it.

I would philosophize on why other women held themselves back in relationships so they wouldn't outgrow their partner. I regarded it as an epidemic. I just couldn't own how I'd found many ways to do that myself over the years. This was my blind spot. Or one of them, at least.

If clear intentions are made, your Higher Power will be there to deliver. However, there are conscious intentions that are actively chosen and unconscious intentions that are derived from fear and loss. My back injury was the manifestation of a conscious intention (helping me leave the Foundation) combined with an unconscious intention (I didn't want to outgrow my man). This was a recipe for something powerful to intervene and put me on another course.

Weeks had passed and I still could not sit. Datta took up a collection from our Ashland community of friends to fly me back home. Within a few weeks, Datta, with help from my dear friend Kim, had raised the money to come over to England and escort me back home on a lie-down flight. I couldn't believe how many people cared for me until I saw the list of contributors on an oversized get-well card. Datta was my white knight on a rescue mission. He was proud to do it. When I saw him pass through the arrival gates of the Newcastle airport, I laughed and cried at the same time. I was so happy yet so beaten up. He kissed me gently on the mouth and with a gentle embrace whispered in my ear, "Everything is going to be okay now."

Being around Datta did make everything feel okay. Even on the days we fell into petty arguments I felt protected. We were sometimes caught in a frustrating loop. He got uptight at how defensive I was when he didn't approve of something I did. I judged him as oversensitive and trying to control me and his environment. I'd never had an argument with a boyfriend before, and it would unsettle me for days. As the relationship got more serious, I became more fearful of being left. Abandonment had always been my fate, and part of me was preparing for it to happen again. That feeling made me want to guard my heart. I could not stand the thought of being so open and have it ripped out of my grasp again.

One day after coming home to Ashland and figuring out a lopsided position I could sit in, I was driving alone along the main boulevard through town. I felt fear because my heart felt so vulnerable and I sensed it closing in relationship to Datta because I didn't want to feel this vulnerable, as he might leave. The Love Dog in me cried out, *I can't live and love this way. I can't guard my heart like this, but I am scared it will not last.*

I then had a powerful realization:

This relationship is going to end. It will cause great pain for one or both of us. It will end in a few weeks, a few months, a few years, or in a few decades with one of us passing away. It's inevitable, so just know it's coming and love like you've never loved before. You are going to hurt at some point along that timeline, but it's more painful to avoid fully giving love because you are scared of losing it.

It was such a powerful realization that I still remember the full bloom of summer and landscaped lawns of Southern Oregon University passing on my right, and my favorite breakfast place, Morning Glory, on my left. I rolled my window down to feel the warm breeze on my arm and committed to giving myself to this relationship unguarded, until whenever the relationship ended.

Everything is temporary, I reminded myself. I want to be as present as I can and enjoy each moment as much as possible.

CHAPTER 26

THE CUT

While in constant pain, I tried to do as much work for the Foundation as my body would allow. I had to keep working to keep money coming in and to be able to stay in the country. My visa only allowed me to work for one specific company and that was with Paul and Jim at CWG Coaching Services, whose only client was the Foundation.

I convinced them I could immediately return to part-time work if I could work from home. I set up my office on Datta's queen-size bed. The arrangement wasn't nearly as sexy as it sounds. I would lie down with a few pillows under my hips to hold my back at just the right angle, my computer at my face with a heat pack on my neck to minimize tension, and ice packs on my back to minimize the spasms. My mobile phone, pen, and Post-it Notes lay beside me on the comforter.

Some days I was glad to have work to distract from the discomfort that continually radiated throughout my body. Some days my positive attitude lasted an hour before I went back to feeling sorry for myself. One day I literally fell asleep in mid-call with a client until my snoring woke me up. As much as I wanted to start my own business, now was not the right time. I rarely had enough energy to work a few hours from bed, let alone speak at local events, shoot promotional videos, and enroll people in my new workshops.

Datta had invited me to move permanently into his house. He happily let me force my way in, as I'd leave an item there every time I visited. We hadn't spent a day apart since my rescue from England, so by now a third of my toiletries were lining his bathroom sink and plenty of clothes were lining his bedside table drawer. I felt more secure of our longevity given that he wanted to live with me so soon into the relationship. At the same time I remembered Tej's words of wisdom: to not give everything away too soon. This was the first time in my life I'd lived with someone I was involved with. We got to know each other very quickly—both what we liked and what we didn't.

Back at the offices of the Foundation, a new executive director had been announced while I was in England. Marion called me to share her exiting news.

"I'm the boss," she said, half joking and half dead serious.

I was happy for her. At least for a week. Then she started to call or email me once a day to ask me to hand over all my work and details on the Leadership program I ran.

"I can take that over while you are in recovery," she said.

I wanted everyone to stay out of my domain so they wouldn't screw it up. I explained in a nice way, "We're in a lull right now since the next intake does not start for another six months, so there is nothing to worry about right now. Customer service can look after the existing students, I can be on all the training calls, and I'll be ready to fill the next group soon enough."

Marion was hired to make the Foundation profitable. I had not seen a year where they didn't have to lay people off. I never worried for my job, given that my program made most of the Foundation's income. Marion made quick decisions, cut costs, and pissed people off left and right. However, revenue from all programs, as well as fund-raising, kept falling no matter what she did.

Most of the staff concluded we needed a leader outside the Inner Circle who had more understanding about finances. I agreed. As soon as she took control, she changed. Later, Datta, who also knew her well, commented, "She didn't change; she just changed the way she related to you."

As the saying goes, you really get to know what someone is like when you give them power. She was the dictator type and her position of power made her show her colors.

I began believing someone unstable was at the helm. I sensed she was worried that her golden goose was no longer able to lay big fat eggs for her anymore. I was her biggest cost as the most expensive person on the team, yet I felt secure, knowing that because of my history at the Foundation, no one would let her fire me.

A month after my return, Marion arrived at the house un-announced with Paul, my visa sponsor.

I hobbled to open the front door to see Paul's smile and Marion looking down at her briefcase.

"Come on in. Do you want tea?"

"No, it's okay," Paul answered for the both of them.

Marion had not looked me in the eye yet as she took a seat on the couch.

She leaned her briefcase against her leg and said, "This is your last day. We are letting you go as of immediately. I brought Paul as a witness to this."

My body went numb while I tried to figure out what this meant.

"Do you mean that you are not even going to give a week's notice?"

"Yes. This is your last day. I'm going to need to collect your computer now."

I asked again, with more bite, "You're not going to give me any time to hand off the running of the biggest, most intricate program we have or let me say goodbye to some of our longest clients?"

"No."

Paul softly interjected, "Where is your computer? I need to get it right now."

I didn't want to say it. "It's in my bedroom on the bed."

I was in shock. I couldn't believe what was happening.

He stood up and left us alone. I wanted to see what was behind Marion's eyes. Any remorse? Her eyes were vacant. I heated up from the inside. At one time we were closest confidantes, but now it made me sick to look at her.

Neale had not been part of the leadership team of the non-profit Foundation for that year. He had more books to write and speaking tours to fulfill. He had stated clearly, "You guys need to sink or swim without me." He did, however, know about Marion's decision before she arrived at my doorstep. Marion had told all the staff what was going to happen and to not answer any communication I made with them. She instructed them not to pick up the phone if they could see it was me, and if I did get through, to hang up on me without a word. She said it was for legal reasons. After I had a day to digest what had happened, I called Joanna and Patty—no response. I called Julia—no response. Dead silence. I had never experienced the fire of anger so intensely. The entire CWG staff, which felt like family, followed her word and cut me off overnight.

She legally did not have to give me any notice or severance. I pleaded over email for a small severance after six years of service and millions of dollars' worth of revenue I produced. *No* was Marion's response. I had told some of our clients and friends of mine how I was unfairly dismissed, which made her furious.

"You're not getting a single penny. You should have kept your mouth shut," she wrote.

I pleaded again via email to my closer friends on the Foundation team to respond to my request to have a conversation to help me get some closure. No response.

It is ironic that when I was abruptly let go, Neale was the only one who reached out to me. He agreed to talk and help me find emotional closure. He invited me up to his new home, which overlooked the valley. We had afternoon tea in front of the big scenic windows as he said why Marion had it in for me. Apparently, I triggered her insecurities in a big way. He shared from his higher perspective why it was time for me to move on. He could see I wanted bigger things, and I couldn't disagree. His wisdom soothed the anger and betrayal that had built up. He thanked me for everything I had done and offered support on the next part of my journey. We had never been friends before, and in those final moments I felt like we had become friends for the first time.

"Thank you for everything you have done for me and the Foundation. If there is any way I can support you in your next phase, let me know. I could give you an introduction to my agent, as I know you will write a book or two," he offered.

He had offered me so much opportunity over the years. I left with respect. Even with all his faults, to his credit, he knew what they were. It's why when I hear someone say something negative about him these days, I'm likely to defend him.

My back pain was excruciating most days, but it taught me a huge lesson. The body, mind, and soul will always find the path of least resistance to put you back on your divine path. At the time I blamed Marion, who wanted me gone. But looking back, the firing was all my creation. I had received ideas for my new business. I had people willing to support me when I made the move. Paul had agreed to sponsor me for a work visa so I could find a way to legally make enough money to support myself. The future was all lined up for me, but month after month, year after year, I'd kept saying no to myself. *No, I'm scared. No, I'm not ready. No, security of a paycheck is more important. No, what if something bad happens?* When you are not in flow in your life, your body will tell you. I spent two years in physical hell contemplating that wisdom.

CHAPTER 27

SURRENDER

In the middle of the night, a blast of physical pain greeted me with a force that was as debilitating as I'd experienced during those first few nights in England. I opened the top drawer of the bedside table only to find the plastic tube of Vicodin pills empty. I maneuvered myself out of bed and to the bathroom cabinet that stored my backup medication. As I rifled through pill bottles and tubes, some fell into the basin and some to the floor.

Fuck, where is it? It's got to be here.

I shuffled to the kitchen cabinet, which offered only non-prescription wussy painkillers. Tylenol was not going to save me, but I downed three and hoped for the best. I maneuvered myself to the sofa, because I had figured out a way to position my back to somewhat relieve the pressure on the nerves causing the mind-numbing pain. If I curved my back in a particular way so that my head and butt were pointing up and my lower back was dipped down, I could at least stand the pain enough to stay conscious. I was moaning as if I was in labor, and that woke Datta up. He came and sat beside me. We had been dating 18 months at that point.

"What can I do, Sweetie? Would a light massage help?"

With tears streaming down my face and panting like I was in a Lamaze class, I said to him, "I cannot do this anymore. I can't do it one more night. I am done. I want you to put a gun to my head and put me out of my misery. There is no way out of this. I feel like I am at the height of pain in labor, but I know there is no end. Please put me out of my misery."

My doctor was initially optimistic that within two years I'd experience a full recovery without surgery. He said year one's focus was to recover more range of movement quickly enough to become functional again so I wouldn't have to go through surgery. I did everything the doctor told me; I went to chiropractic care three times per week. I altered my diet to stop inflammation. I cut soy, gluten, dairy, and eggs. Since I was already a vegetarian, this sparked the occasional sarcastic remark about how all I could eat now was lettuce. I would always force a giggle for them even though I thought they were an idiot.

In hindsight, my back represented an unconscious test to see if Datta would stick around. I have wondered if he would have stayed with me if I was fully able to look after myself. He is a natural provider and protector. He is loyal—some would say to a fault. As much as I admired his commitment, I had doubts. Was his honor and loyalty kicking in rather than love for me?

The injury created an outlook that was different from anything ever before. I had to become dependent, which I don't do well on the best of days. I didn't have anyplace else to go. Datta showed incredible patience. He never once said how much he suffered seeing me that way when he could do little about it. He only showed me that I could count on him. His loyalty inspired me to rethink how I felt about love. Real love sticks around. Real love doesn't leave. I was slowly getting that not all guys are more in love with their freedom than intimacy, the depth of which comes from a genuinely committed relationship. I chose to focus on the tender healing of his touch and the way he took pride in keeping me safe. Our love continually grew stronger.

I was usually transported to doctors and chiropractic visits in the back of Datta's minivan. He'd removed all the seats and laid down a futon mattress and blankets. That van became my ambulance. Usually I was on all fours like a dog, bending my back to take the pressure off. I could now lie flat on my back for up to an hour; the problem was, I couldn't get up without screaming. To raise myself to the upright position I would have to pinch a bunch of nerves. The three seconds of torture was sometimes worth the trade-off of an hour on my back, but in the minivan I chose to remain panting like a dog on all fours, waiting for the ride to end.

Dr. Logan, my first chiropractor, had an open floor plan office. Beyond the front desk, you could see a few patients being adjusted and some using the rehabilitation machines. I felt vulnerable, as this modern maze of equipment afforded no privacy. Dr. Logan was one of the most generous, caring men you could meet. He'd helped one of Datta's friends recover from an extreme neck injury. The biggest problem was that I couldn't stand any pressure and very little movement, and his style of chiropractic employed a lot of manual adjustments. I tried to hold in my agony. I wanted to tell him I was getting better, but I wasn't. I didn't want to say much at all, because he was so sweet and empathetic that if I really let myself feel how much he cared, I would have broken down crying in front of him and I didn't want to do that in public.

One day I had to speak up. I was in the middle of an adjustment position, and pain ricocheted through my entire body. "I can't do this. Please, I need to get off the table. Move out of the way!" I almost shouted as if my life depended on it.

I pulled myself off the adjustment table and rolled onto the floor in seconds. I resumed the all-fours panting dog position. There was nowhere to hide. I lost any semblance of dignity I had left as I sobbed into the coarse carpet under my hands and knees. Dr. Logan and everyone else in the office stopped still in silence, like they were paying their respects to someone who had just passed. I could feel the sympathy coming from all directions. On the next visit, they had flipped one of the offices into a private room for me.

I would eventually feel some relief, but I didn't know which of the therapies I was undergoing made the biggest difference. Within a year I was able to stand a light massage every few weeks, which also helped relieve the constant muscle spasm that had me bent over to my right side to protect the left, where my body had betrayed me. I woke up one morning of a scheduled massage and felt stabbing in my lower back and left leg. I had Kim pick me up in her car, as Datta had already left in the van for the day. I sat up in the front seat, holding onto the handle at the top of the passenger door to keep the pressure off my back. It got worse with every intersection we passed. We pulled up on A Street, outside one of the restored historic homes that had been turned into office space for therapists and healers.

As soon as we came to a complete stop, I pulled myself out of the car and fell directly onto the sidewalk. I resumed my most consistent position when the mind-numbing pain hit. There I was, on all fours again, sobbing again, trying to not move again, and blocking foot traffic. A few passersby tried to stop and help.

"Tell them to go away. I don't want anyone seeing me like this."

I was mortified. My butt was high in the air for everyone to see.

Kim bent down and asked, "Can we help you try to get up into the house so your massage therapist can help with stretching you out?"

"No, don't touch me! Just get me something to put under my knees," I urged.

I couldn't rise off the sidewalk from my all-fours position for half an hour. My massage therapist, Carol, sat beside me on the sidewalk as I wept. We all knew the process. The emergency room was not going to be able to do anything except give me a reprieve for a day. The bathroom cabinet was again full of medication, which was just a Band-Aid.

I rarely saw anyone other than Datta and a few close friends. I didn't want people to see me when I was so helpless, stuck in the prison of my body. On the occasional better day, I would ride in the back of the minivan, and Datta drove us to Five Rhythms Dance on a Sunday morning for some free-form dance. Datta was a dancer, for sure. Tej was right. Women would line up to dance with him. Literally. That just made me prouder to be the one he went home with.

I'd dance in my corner and the group knew to be careful not to bump into me. I'd ground my energy through my legs, close my eyes, and start to feel the sensuality in the slowest, subtlest of hip circles. The micro-movements would send joy to my heart and a slight smile to my face. I pushed the range of movement a little more, as I longed to dance again, but I would quickly end up behind the curtain at the end of the dance space, breathing through the pain. I almost always vowed never to return because it was a reminder of what everyone else had and what I didn't— the ability to move and to enjoy that movement.

Year two was spent trying to figure out why I wasn't improving much. It was still hard to take any physical pressure from Datta's hands as he tried to ease the severity of the spasms. I had decided to change chiropractors after feeling traumatized every time I heard the snap, crack, or pop of a physical adjustment. The tension that the crack could relieve was canceled out by the trauma in my mind, which tightened every last muscle to defend against the next crack.

I went to Gary Ferguson again and asked him to test through his kinesiology what sort of healing was supportive to my body and what wasn't. He tested every single chiropractic, osteopathic, physiotherapeutic, and somatic system he knew about, which totaled hundreds. The only method that tested strong was the B.E.S.T (which stands for Bio-Energetic Synchronization Technique) system of chiropractic, which I had not previously heard of. With that knowledge I found my second chiropractor, Dr. Welch, who practiced an hour away from us in Grants Pass. It was worth two hours in the car for a 30-minute session three times a week. I started experiencing relief immediately. Without physical manipulation and with more of an energetic focus, I didn't leave traumatized and saw improvement in results.

More was needed than healing my body. It didn't matter if I had a good week or bad. Every time I felt pain, it sent the message to my brain that I was not getting better. I found myself telling others I wasn't healing and asking the question, "Why am I not healing?" even though I did experience improvement, finally. I did not yet understand that these thoughts were maintaining the pattern of not healing. My dominant thoughts were in the realm of, *This is hell,* or *When will this end?* or *I am hurting,* or *I am depressed and can't get out of this mess.* My attention was constantly focused on what I didn't want. I would say that I wanted healing, but I couldn't access the feeling of being healed. I was stuck in the situation versus realizing the ability to access my potential future. I understood in concept that the release of pain begins to happen when internal stillness and acceptance is achieved. Only in a state of non-resistance could I advance to a new reality, yet I was nowhere near perceiving this wisdom.

On my 237th visit to the chiropractor (yes, I kept count), I lay on the adjusting table and looked up at compassionate and wise Dr. Welch. It was a dark day following yet another agonizing setback. He stopped his treatment and looked at me with kind eyes. In a soft voice he said, "It may be time to consider surgery."

Tears welled up and my head started to shake. *No, no. What are you saying?* I said to myself. All sorts of fearful thoughts took over.

I don't have health insurance in this country. If I had surgery, I would have to fly all the way back to Australia for the procedure and I'd be away from Datta and my closest friends for a long time. I couldn't afford to take another year to recover from surgery.

I had already spent two years in hell. Dr. Welch took the chair beside me and said, "Just mull over the possibility. If it gives you your life back, it's worth considering."

The intensity of my inner reaction was the clear signal I was in deep resistance to the pain that was happening to me. I have always believed in the saying, "What you resist persists," but never had I heard those words so clearly as on the trip home from Dr. Welch.

For the next week, I spent many hours in prayer and contemplation, asking myself, *Would I be okay if I were in chronic pain for the rest of my life? Would I be okay if nothing ever changed?* I knew I had to find a way to look at my situation with new eyes if I was going to be able to let go of the fear and resistance that had such a hold on me. I played various scenes of possibilities on the screen of my imagination. I could use voice-recognition software that would take dictation, which would save me from sitting at my desk too long. I could teach more of the workshops I was starting in tele-seminar format rather than in person. And even though my social life would look different, I imagined holding great parties at home so my friends could come to me rather than me go to them.

I prayed for the strength and courage to know that I could face anything life threw at me, and I gave up my mental and emotional struggle with my back. I gave up resistance. I allowed myself to become okay with the pain. It didn't happen overnight, but within a few days I started to feel my body and heart soften as I heard my own soothing answer: Yes, I would be okay. If nothing ever changed, I could still live a happy life and do my work in the world. I would find a way. Within a few weeks after that, without surgery, I was almost completely pain free. It was a miracle. A miracle because of the physical change, and a miracle because the experience of letting go of control had a profound spiritual impact on my life.

Many people are confused by what spiritual surrender really means. It does not mean giving up on our dreams or our intentions. We must always choose what we want. We are still in the driver's seat when deciding on our life's direction. Surrender is about letting go of our strategic mind and surrendering into partnership with our Higher Power. We also have to give up the need to know how and when something will happen. It's crazy to think we can see the whole picture from our narrow vantage point. We can only see a small part of the picture at any time. Our Higher Power sees the whole picture. As in the team-building game of Trust, someone is in front of you, about to push you, and another is behind to catch you before you fall. You can't see if the person is behind you or has deserted you; you are placing your well-being in the hands of someone else. Surrender is about placing the outcome in the hands of something more powerful than the small you.

I realized the only way to get out of my prison was to master the mind-body-spirit connection. My surrender and almost spontaneous healing was an exponential leap forward in unlocking my cells. Resistance is an energy I now try to notice inside of myself daily. Resistance shows up as a negative emotional charge when something is happening that I don't want. When I feel this resistance, I move in the opposite direction of the Divine path that has been laid out for me. I praise the feeling of resistance these days, because it sends me the message I'm going the wrong way. It has not been easy to surrender my resistance, but along with stilling my mind with meditation and doing my Shadow Work, I believe it's a necessary part of my path to enlightenment.

I now know without a doubt that whatever you resist gets harder. Whatever you worry about sticks to you. And if you surrender, with courage and arms wide open, you will experience the magnitude of who you are and true liberation. That is a power that nobody, no situation, no bad economy, and no political leader can take away from you.

Friends, the Beloved is a lion,
We are a deer that has a bad leg and can't run.
Cornered, with no way to escape, in those arms,
the most we can do is give up.
~ RUMI

• CHAPTER 28 •

TWO FIRES

The end of the nightmare was in sight, and love had lasted.

My family adored Datta. Without any of them saying a word, I knew they all thought he couldn't be more perfect for me. He kept them laughing. Datta loved playing jokes on them, especially my mum, which increased their affection for him even more.

One Christmas Eve, Datta and I decided to head out of town to a bed and breakfast in a dense Oregon forest. When we arrived, we realized we'd hit the jackpot—no other guests had booked a room for the next three days. The owners left us the keys, instructions on how things worked, plenty of dry wood for the open fireplace—and the entire property to ourselves. The setting was so remote, our cell phones did not work, so we had told Mum to call us at the inn's number at a particular time so we could wish everyone there a Merry Christmas. She called right on time. Datta had a mischievous look on his face as he picked up the phone at the reception desk. There was an extension phone on the other side of the room that I picked up as well.

"Howdy," he said in the most southern drawl he could muster.

"Hello, may I speak to Rachael Jayne?" my mum politely asked in very proper Australian English.

"There ain't no gal here by that name. I think you got the wrong number, ma'am," he said as his drawl got even thicker.

"Is this the Cascade Mountain Inn?" Mum asked.

"Yes, ma'am, but there ain't no gal here by that name, as I already said."

I was silently laughing with my hand over my mouth because his accent was hilarious and I wondered where he was going with this charade.

"I know my daughter is staying there. She's with a man named Datta," she said.

"Datta! What kind of a name is that?"

She giggled.

Datta sighed theatrically. "Can you describe what she looks like, ma'am?"

"Yes, certainly. She's tall and has auburn hair," Mum said.

"Aw-burn! What on Earth is aw-burn, ma'am?" I could hear Mum giggling and suspected she was thinking, *This guy is stupid.*

Her nervous laughter picked up its pace and volume. We could hear her say to everyone in the background, "This man doesn't know what auburn means."

Mum was an elegant, articulate, prim and proper kind of woman who never wanted anyone to feel bad about themselves, so she tried her hardest to stop laughing at this guy on the phone while Datta kept saying in his hilarious Southern accent, "What are you laughing at, ma'am? Are you laughing at me, ma'am? I don't think that is very nice."

She couldn't stop giggling like a 10-year-old girl, and knowing Mum, she would have been mortified that she couldn't stop herself.

"Now, hold your horses there," Datta said. "Is she the one that talks funny? And she got red hair?"

"Yes, yes, yes! She's the one that talks funny! And she has aub—red hair."

"Well, then, why didn't you just say so?" He then made a show of putting the phone down to go look for me.

She was still laughing as I took the phone. "My goodness, Rachael Jayne, what kind of place are you staying at?

I couldn't contain my laughter and told her that had been Datta all along. The whole family was in hysterics when she told them.

This out-of-control giggling habit came upon her at interesting times. One day she was pulled over by an intimidating policeman because one of her taillights was out. In Australia it's standard procedure to give everyone a breath test to see if they have alcohol in their bloodstream. Mum always knew the most appropriate thing to do and she did it. I only heard her swear under her breath twice in her entire life. She rarely drank alcohol.

"May I see your license, please?" the tall, mustached police-man demanded as he stood over her at the car window. "Have you had any alcohol today?"

"No, I have not."

"Blow into this tube for me." He handed her a breath-test device.

She looked at it nervously, put it up to her mouth, and took the biggest suck she could, as if she was sucking a milkshake.

"That is not a breath, Mrs. Kennedy," said the policeman. "That is you sucking air from the tube. I need you to blow into it."

"Oh gosh, I'm so sorry," she said with a giggle.

She put the tube up to her mouth again. Her brain said blow and her mouth sucked.

"No, do not suck, Mrs. Kennedy. Blow!" he said, agitated.

It took her three tries in between giggles to get it right while I sat in the passenger seat, trying not to laugh and make it worse for her. It was hilarious.

The device reported alcohol in her blood.

"How much alcohol have you consumed today, Mrs. Kennedy?"

"I haven't consumed any alcohol—today or any time this month," she said.

"That can't be true, Mrs. Kennedy; your breath test has come back positive."

In that moment she started her Diane Kennedy giggle and couldn't stop. She'd realized that she'd been taking cough medicine on a regular basis over the past few days and it probably had alcohol in it. She couldn't stop giggling as she tried to communicate that she'd been consuming cough medicine.

"How much alcohol have you consumed today, Mrs. Kennedy?" he repeated impatiently, looking over at my reaction.

"None," she giggled.

The policeman wasn't amused.

In the passenger seat, I was trying hard not to catch the giggle bug, as that would have set Mum over the edge.

"I have this nervous giggle problem," she spat out.

We both burst out laughing.

Somehow after Mum convinced him that it was cough medicine that created the alcohol reading, he let us go. The cop, however, did not think we were funny.

Now Datta was making her laugh in the same way. I wanted a man to choose me. I wanted my knight in shining armor on his trusty steed to ride up to me and proclaim, *You are the only woman for me!* I had plenty of experiences of the opposite— boys, guys, and some men liking me, even possibly loving me, but not enough to choose me. I'm a romantic, so the greatest pain came when I was not chosen.

My heart ached for a man of my dreams to look at me with total focus and say, "You're everything I want. You're the most extraordinary woman I've ever met and I'm never leaving."

This longing rubbed up against the feminist part of me that loved reading and listening to Naomi Wolf and Alanis Morrissette, but the desire was always there—clear, wanted, and unspoken.

I had found that man of my dreams in Datta. It's like having the most loving, nurturing, protective foundation underneath you that makes you know without a doubt that everything is going to be okay. The foundation he created for me can almost be described as a godlike presence in my life. It's like the feeling you get when you know there is a Higher Power lighting up the path for you to experience even more love, joy, and abundance. His presence helped me almost entirely clear out the residue of anxiety in my solar plexus, which has been a close companion for my whole life. That foundation gave me the impetus to just go for it. I felt there was nothing I couldn't do when I had him in my corner.

He's my bodyguard. He doesn't let anyone who could hurt me get too close. He's always had one eye on the amazing work he does and one eye on me. Not in a weak, she-needs-me kind of way. It's his masculine, protective instinct. He doesn't just guard my body, but my heart and mind as well. He's always there to challenge a limiting belief or a less-than-loving thought I have about myself.

He's a nurturer. It helped that among many other qualities he trained as a master chef. The love that I can literally taste in his hot organic vegetarian dishes and delicious smoothies makes me sigh. It helps that he used to work as a masseuse and has magic hands. The relief to my body when he decides to give his attention to it creates more than just a sigh. It helps that he is a MacGyver. He seems capable of fixing anything around the home or in the car with some string, a tube of toothpaste, and a match. It helps that he is a comedian. The belly laughs he causes are a constant source of lightness and have saved me when I really needed them.

We have often commented how easy it is to be around each other, because we allow each other to be exactly who we are. That's not an easy feat given the intensity of our personalities.

Datta is kind, generous, intelligent, hilarious, goofy, romantic, fun, spiritually connected, affectionate, creative, wise, intuitive, sensitive, reassuring, handsome, and passionately intense in all the right ways. I hit the love jackpot.

I followed the Divine Breadcrumbs, the path lit up, and there he was.

I had proclaimed to friends thousands of times that I did not want to get married because I didn't want to adopt society's definition of this social structure. Oprah and Stedman weren't married. Susan Sarandon and Tim Robbins weren't married. Gary Zukav and his partner Linda Francis weren't married. I saw it somehow as a higher choice to not get married, and instead have what Gary called a "Spiritual Partnership." Commitment was important to me, but marriage seemed outdated.

On February 15th, 2008, Datta asked me to marry him. He gave my parents a shock when he called them in Australia first and asked permission to take their firstborn daughter's hand in marriage. He was sneaky to wait all through Valentine's Day to surprise me. It didn't cross my mind that he was going to propose, so when he sat on the couch beside me in silence, I didn't know what he was up to. I had pushed the couch as close to the fireplace as I could. I was wrapped and cozy in my pink fluffy dressing gown, with breakfast on my lap and enjoying the radiant heat.

"What?" I asked, knowing he was up to some kind of mischief. "What are you looking at me like that for?"

He looked at me with his deep-set eyes and simply said, "Will you marry me?"

I knew this was not an easy decision for him, as he'd sworn he would never marry again. This time, apparently, he knew he had finally found the right woman, and that morning he was eager to surprise me with the question that he never dreamed he'd be asking again. As I realized what was being asked, I was transported into a different reality and didn't know what to say other than "Yes. Of course." It was the easiest answer for me. In a flash my judgment about marriage vaporized. How the reality of being in love changed so many things.

There we were, melting into each other's arms, close to two fires—one in the fireplace and the other from our love.

The moment reminded me of a poem that Datta had written about our love in the first month of our relationship.

We can never fully understand love.
We can only move a bit closer to the fire,
and warm our cold hands.
Your fire warms me in ways I can feel,
but not even hope to describe.

As we reminisced about the beginnings of our love affair, I was struck by the perfection of the journey. I had been delayed seven days in my attempt to get back to Ashland to see Robert. As much as I wanted other relationships at the time and would have done everything in my power to make them work, my Higher Power knew all along who and what it was leading me to. The timeline and agenda my Higher Power had was not the same as what my ego tried to push. Now engaged to my soul mate, I knew that all those days and nights of impatience, worry, and stress that love would never find me were a waste of energy.

We both wanted a short engagement so we wouldn't waste a year of our lives on decisions about colors, dresses, menus, and flower arrangements. Our business together was finally gathering momentum that we didn't want to stop. The YIN Project had its first successful Feminine Spirituality and Leadership Program, and Datta's speaker workshops had risen in attendance.

During the preparation for the wedding, I had almost full range of movement in my back and was able to perform light daily exercise.

"You're better because you chose to marry me," Datta would say, half joking.

I felt better on so many levels.

On the afternoon of the day before the wedding, our families converged on our home to start the introductions over finger food and flowers. I had decided to save money by arranging our own bouquets, which were now displayed all over the kitchen table. My well-behaved clean-cut Aussie family met Datta's eccentric family. His mum was delightful. The eccentricity started with her and her oversized colorful glasses and bubbly personality. Always talking, she was in heaven as she met her new family. Datta is one of five genius-level boys who were not admired for their social skills as much as the intellectual, artistic, and mathematical recognition they'd achieved throughout their lives. As I held my bouquet and my sister tied a pale pink ribbon around it, I started feeling those familiar painful twinges on the left side of my lower back. By that evening they had become full-blown spasms that caused me to bow out of the pre-wedding festivities and head straight to bed with ice packs, painkillers, and a strong dose of anxiety. I couldn't believe the timing. I was supposed to be staying at a friend's loft to experience the tradition of not seeing my husband until the ceremony. Instead I lay beside Datta in our bed as we both tried to not think about what the next day would bring if I wasn't able to walk down the aisle.

I woke up the next day feeling hopeful as I stretched my back out before getting out of bed. Within an hour I was screaming for Datta to find me as much pain medication as we had. I downed the largest dose I could right before I was taken to the hairdresser and then to my friend's house where I was to primp and get dressed. All morning I couldn't imagine myself getting through the day. The last thing I wanted was 80 guests worrying about me when they should be admiring my dress. It took me twice as long as a normal bride (who is always fashionably late) to get to the wedding site. Trying to maneuver into my ivory beaded traditional corseted wedding dress and doing my own makeup was a challenge when I couldn't sit or stand up straight.

I finally arrived at the stunning garden setting in Lithia Park just by the creek. By the time my dad started to walk me down the grassy aisle, I was drugged up to my eyeballs and had a big smile on my face. Datta came into view with his two handsome sons beside him as his best men. All three of them, who had never been dressed in three-piece tuxedos, were sweltering in the humid 108-degree heat, even under the shade of the two massive oak trees that umbrellaed the congregation. I knew they were losing pounds under the wool—for me. I was the one who wanted to wear the traditional wedding dress with a train. I wanted the suits. I wanted the matching color theme of olive green and pale pink. I stood before Datta, my family, my community, Mother Nature, and God. We'd had two years of undeniable love and compatibility, and when we shared our vows we knew that the commitment we were making would last a lifetime. I have never been more certain of anything in my life.

Thankfully, the Vicodin and the corset, combined with the awe of marrying the man of my dreams, kept me "high" enough that day that I was able to make it through. We arrived at the modest Ashland community center for the reception just before an auspicious downpour and weather strong enough to blow some of the old windows open. I unhooked my train, hugged my friends, and danced the night away in front of a four-piece band between speeches by our parents. They all had everyone laughing at our expense and moved by their pride in us. Datta carried me over the threshold of our hotel room entrance that night, and by noon the following day I could not walk.

We had planned a "wedding reception number 2" for that afternoon for our many friends who were not invited to the wedding. We were both connected to so many large communities in town that we decided to have a smaller wedding for family and close friends and a larger party the next day. It started at six that evening. It took me two hours to get out of bed, get dressed, get into the car, drive ten minutes across town, and get out of the car and into the venue. I had never been so immobile, even on the worst of days in London. I couldn't even do my usual wobbly walk. Datta gave me more pills and a cup of water, and he became my brace. As long as I had my arm around his neck and shoulder and the weight of my upper body didn't connect with my back, I could stand the pain. If he let me go, the pain was unbearable. There we were in the center of an 80-person circle of love that was drowning us in verbal blessings and speeches. I could hardly see through the watery fog of my contact lenses, but inside I was experiencing perfection. I had my man by my side and love beaming all around me.

For the next two weeks, I could not walk, stand up on my own, or sit down on a chair. I was either in bed with hot packs and ice packs in their specific positions or peeing standing up in the shower. Instead of spending time exploring the wilderness with my family (who had traveled all the way from Australia) and preparing for our honeymoon, I was doing anything and everything I could think of to deal with the pain. They would take turns sitting by my bed and sharing how great the ceremony was, and I asked them about news from back home. The miracle was, even with all the pain, these were some of the happiest weeks I can remember. I was okay with what was happening because I wasn't resisting it. I was okay with the prospect that I might experience these intense pains forever. And, like the tides, the pain came in, and then the pain went out. I was grateful that this period of pain was shorter than any other.

Years later I am in great health. I wear lower heels and don't carry heavy bags up flights of stairs on my own. I've had a few spells of pain that lasted a few days each. But each episode taught me something very specific and led me to experience something important. These days I thank my back for being my best reminder of when I am not letting Grace guide me on the road I am meant to be on and when I am resisting the flow of my own life. It's my teacher now. The memories keep me humble.

CHAPTER 29

THE ART OF FEMININE
PRESENCE

Divine Breadcrumbs led me to Ashland, and they were about to lead me to my next home as a newlywed. Ashland was safe and small, but the culture had become more irritating than inspiring. Datta and I felt suffocated. I could not walk through the co-op without seeing at least three people I felt I had to talk to. I had trouble differentiating what I wanted to offer to the world amongst all the wannabe thought leaders who lived among many of the world-renowned thought leaders. How could I carve out my own space?

We decided to sell Datta's home in order to survive on our smaller incomes and high credit card balances. I sold my wedding dress and whatever else I didn't need. The need to economize didn't stem from a lifestyle that had gotten out of control. It was the aftermath of medical bills and the fact we were trying to build a new business without much forward progress. Week after week no offers came in for the house. We kept dropping the price, then dropping it more. We couldn't move without the sale, so the small-town claustrophobia worsened.

In one of my sessions with Gary, he instructed me to check in with my guidance and ask my body where I should live next. In a flash, out of nowhere, I said, "Colorado." He muscle-tested me and my hand was strong. I thought that was a fluke, so I immediately asked, "Can you check Texas and Arizona?"

"They are both weak," Gary reported.

"What about New York or New Jersey?"

"Both are weak."

"Canada?"

"Weak."

"Australia?"

"Weak."

Every place I threw at Gary produced a weak response in my body with the muscle test.

"Colorado?"

"Strong."

When we visited Colorado for the first time, Datta and I made a decision to do what we called "The Whole Foods Test." We sat in every store on the Front Range of the Rocky Mountains, and over our staple veggie sushi and balsamic beet salad we felt the energy of the locals as they gathered their weekly organics in their baskets. On a folded-out paper map we had drawn a red circle from southern Denver all the way north to Longmont. A few weeks before we left to visit, I heard my inner voice say out of the blue, "Make sure you check out Fort Collins, too." I got the red sharpie out again and expanded the circle on the map.

All bets were on Boulder. There was a lot of consciousness work there and a lot of Ashlanders told us we'd love it. When we arrived at the Boulder Whole Foods, we were amazed by all the good-looking, fit people in high-end outdoor gear. It seemed too pretentious for our down-to-earth nature and a lot like Ashland—with more style and money. I got anxious every day we were in Boulder because I had truly thought it would be our next home, but neither of us wanted to move there. After three days Boulder ended up a clear no.

We'd already checked out multiple areas in and around Denver and found nothing close to what we wanted. Fort Collins was the last spot on the list, and so we hit the only Whole Foods Market there for lunch. Within fifteen minutes we knew we had found our new hometown. The people, the energy, the place—everything fit. I looked over at the people in the checkout line and the cashiers behind the registers—everyone was smiling. I was struck by the overwhelming notion that people loved living there.

Datta walked up to a cute twentysomething college student at the checkout with a purple streak in her hair and asked, "Do you enjoy living here?"

"Oh yeah; Fort Collins is awesome."

Datta kept her laughing before her next customer started to unpack their goods on the belt while I kept looking around at others walking by, eating, drinking their coffee. I had been setting the intention for months prior to the trip to have my body, heart, and soul know without a doubt when I would reach our new home. I kept saying to myself, "I will just know when I am there." That is exactly what happened.

We did not know a soul. Doors opened for us around every turn. We opened a P.O. box before we left and went home to tell all our Ashland friends that we were moving to Colorado right away.

The standard interaction went like this. "Oh, great; Boulder is awesome. You'll love it there."

"No, we are moving to Fort Collins."

"Why Fort Collins?" they'd say as if they thought we were out of our minds moving to a middle-American kind of town. Most of our friends had never heard of the place. We never thought we'd live in the suburbs, with perfectly manicured lawns, concrete sidewalks, and HOA requirements. But with its 300 days of sunshine per year, not much traffic, and happy people, it was the perfect place for us to live. Yet again, if I had used my strategic mind, I wouldn't have chosen such a perfect place.

Mum was ecstatic, because now she "had another excuse to travel." She'd walked the Great Wall of China with my sister, been kissed by a giraffe, and seen the pyramids. Our entire family was healthily addicted to travel. Between the six of us, we'd been to most corners of the globe a few times over. Now almost empty nesters and in their early sixties, Mum and Dad had time for more adventures. They were still both the epitome of health, so a trip to a part of the States they had never visited would be easy to pull off.

We lost Datta's Ashland home to foreclosure after not being able to get our business off the ground quickly enough. Datta was ashamed about packing up the home after this blow. I was ashamed about checks bouncing, having to call the bank to plead with them to reverse overdraft charges, and deal with the financial restrictions that had taken over our lives. At least this was a way we could leave Ashland unencumbered; plus, we had each other and a big adventure ahead of us. Datta left Oregon in the biggest U-Haul truck we could rent with all our belongings, dragging my new lime-green Volkswagen Beetle on the tow bar. Our dog Hannah and I followed in the minivan. We drove across California, Nevada, Utah, Wyoming, and finally into Colorado, having no place to live yet. We decided to stay in the local Super 8 Motel until we could find a place to rent. We lived in that small Super 8 room for three weeks with seven guitars, three suitcases, and a Rottweiler. All the boxes, other suitcases, furniture, and now dead houseplants were parked in the U-Haul in the parking lot. We were greeted by the coldest week in Colorado for 30 years, and while walking our dog in minus 10-degree (Fahrenheit) weather with high winds, we wondered if we had lost our minds.

I was so grateful that I'd heard the divine message "The ground that you live on may not be supporting you." I followed the continuous call to move somewhere else, and it was the exact right move. Datta and I felt almost an instant shift when we moved to Colorado.

It was time to reinvent myself. I was good at that, and I had already proved that moving to new schools, towns, or countries was the best time to do that. No one had any preconceived notion of who I was. Who did I want to be now?

I gave up the casual wear of Ashland and bought the first pencil skirt of my life. I gave up the contentment in genteel poverty that pervades many small towns and started dreaming of earning a good living. I gave up only marketing online and stretched my resistant introverted personality to get out of the house and network and speak to groups about my own work for the first time. I gave up following spiritual teachers and gave myself permission to be the teacher.

At times I became judgmental of my new environment. I judged people as not being as evolved as my old friends. Local teachers and speakers were teaching less refined concepts than I wanted. The internal chatter of superiority soothed me and kept me company. Until one evening while contemplating why I was being so judgmental—it hit me. I was lonely. I again had no friends—except Datta, of course. The physical pain in my heart arrived two seconds after this realization, and before I knew it I was curled in a fetal position and cried myself back down off my high horse. I had witnessed many times before how quickly I shifted from feeling inferior to feeling superior when I felt insecure or like I didn't belong. The slide the other way was a fast and easy ride. I just hadn't seen it as clearly as now. My release that night opened me up, and I started building new important friendships almost immediately.

I felt the impulse to design my own in-person weekly classes and weekend workshop that would help women be seen, heard, and respected more and at the same time accelerate their spiritual awakening while connecting more to their feminine essence. I also wanted a faster way to meet new friends, and I thought this would do the trick.

Six months after arriving in Colorado, I started a class in June 2009 and called it the *Art of Feminine Presence*®. This class was an experiment to see what made a woman more magnetic, more alive, more attractive, and more internally powerful so no one could rock her off her center. I knew it was connected to embodiment and whether they could stay in their pelvis and be present no matter what. It aligned with their energy and how they were using that to attract or repel people. It tapped into their primary sexual essence. It increased the presence in their voice, the courageous way they processed fear, their ability to integrate unconscious Shadows, and be clearer on their intentions.

I was the first guinea pig in the creation cycle of *Art of Feminine Presence*®. I designed a practice that I would do for a week and then I would record how people responded to me. I kept a journal of the responses and noticed how more solid and safe I felt within myself.

I created 22 practices, and they each passed the test. I now knew I didn't have to try so hard to attract the attention I wanted, which was perfect for an introvert who feels drained after being around a lot of people where I felt like I had to be "on." I felt calmer, less self-conscious, and began another quantum leap in my spiritual realization. I could more easily embody the potential of who I wanted to become.

I somehow convinced five women to join me in the first series of *Art of Feminine Presence*® classes, which I held in the living room of our rental home. I found them in random places. One was a Toastmaster acquaintance, one my personal trainer, two women I met at a networking event, and the other my new chiropractor. I led this first class in a series of five two-hour classes once a week. I would teach them a single new practice out of the 22, and then we'd all go out into the world during the week and practice it with others and notice how they responded to us differently. Within a week, they all felt the shift. People started asking them, "What have you been doing?" or "I want what you're having." Within six months, 35 women had found their way to my living room, which I transformed with a few beeswax candles on wooden plates and a red Indian embroidered cloth over the TV screen.

The first five ladies were my favorites. We were all viscerally transforming before each other's eyes, which is why they continued coming to my class each week for an entire year. By that time Lauren, my personal trainer, was leaving for Austin. She stayed after class to tell me, and then she asked what would be a life-altering question for my career: "Would you be open to teaching me how to become a teacher of this work?"

After I contemplated the consequences of this and how much time it would take, I said, "Yes, let's do it." Lauren couldn't have been a more perfect person to be the first one to teach it. When she moved to Austin, she created her own community, which spread quickly. She found teaching *Art of Feminine Presence*® classes a great way to raise a banner that said: Calling all compassionate, conscious, creative women who want to live their Highest Vision.

I held the first teacher training with eight women in our basement. We were now renting in another area of town, and the basement was dark and harder to transform into a delicious space for women to "let go" into their feminine essence. The ugly brown carpet with its gray accent looked like it had 50 cigarette stains. After getting the carpet steam-cleaned for the second time, I had to face the unbelievable fact that the damage had not been caused by stains or burns. It was just a very ugly carpet. With three huge mirrors that Datta hung on the far wall, a rug, and an altar of statues and picture frames and plenty of candles, the space became passable. *You have to start somewhere,* I thought.

Satina was one of the eight who did the teacher training. We hadn't been in contact for years. She was living in the USA but was traveling back and forth to Australia to see her kids. I knew she'd love *Art of Feminine Presence*®, and I wanted her to see all I had accomplished. I felt I'd made it. I was able to run a six-day training with amazing women and be paid for it. I also now had between 8–10 private clients at a time wanting personal coaching to conduct their own feminine leadership journey. The *Art of Feminine Presence*® practices attracted more clients. It also helped me deal with my fear of putting myself out there. Datta and I still couldn't pay all our bills and we were painfully in debt, but it didn't seem to matter as much because I was doing what I loved.

Twenty-two practices turned into 44. The basement changed to a nice workshop room in Fort Collins, and the next year a small ballroom in a hotel and at times stunning international retreat centers. Going from two mini speakers on the side of the TV to a full stage and sound system was heavenly for me. Having hundreds of women experience the power of this work turn into thousands was like a surreal dream with the happiest of endings.

When people ask me why I think *Art of Feminine Presence*® spread across the world so quickly, I can't give a simple answer. One of the biggest reasons is that many women want to feel their own power and value, as well as make changes in their life. You cannot easily change a negative pattern in your life without the power of being witnessed by another.

Let me explain. All the individual habits and patterns of communication that don't serve us are wound up in our relationships to others. For example, your mother may have told you to not be so full of yourself when you shared something you were proud of. Or a stranger gave you creepy sexual attention on a day you felt beautiful and sensual. Perhaps a lover left you at a vulnerable time. Or your speech teacher told you that you were not cut out for standing in front of the room. The lessons are etched in our psyche, so our ego does its job to keep us safe and keep the brakes on, even when we feel the urge to move forward.

When I realized my patterns of feeling unworthy couldn't be changed by reading a book or my fear of speaking to larger audiences couldn't be overcome unless I challenged myself to speak in public, I started to design the 44 practices to unwind the patterns that did not serve women anymore. I knew *Art of Feminine Presence*® had to be built on the foundation of "Being Witnessed." I had to have a group of women with whom I felt safe witness me while I did something I was scared to do. That way the memory of their support overrode the old memories. I have changed so much since 2009, and the biggest reason is that almost every week I have had a group of women give me genuine positive feedback about who they thought I was when I embodied my Feminine Presence and rested in the core of my body.

If a person doesn't understand what I mean by "Being Witnessed," I explain that this work is not just helping women be more feminine, but it can change their subconscious thoughts, increase their magnetic presence, and attract the attention they want. They can own their own value and stand in their truth no matter what. They can melt away any competition and bitchiness with other women that lingers. That way they can remove the brakes and start living up to their full potential. Usually I end the conversation with, "You just have to experience it."

"Look at him," Karen said.

My *Art of Feminine Presence*® sister was pointing to Datta. I turned around, and there he was dancing to Bruno Mars un-apologetically with his arms in the air, surrounded by a circle of women that had formed around him just after finishing one of our *Art of Feminine Presence*® live intensives.

"Not many men would be so comfortable with all these women," she said.

I laughed. "He's not just comfortable; he loves it. He was made for this work."

As I joined the circle, clapping in unison around my man, it struck me that the whole divine experience of putting together these 44 practices and creating *Art of Feminine Presence*® had been born out of my pain.

The pain of not finding true love led me to embody my femininity and make the descent fully into my body. The pain of not being courageous about past decisions led me to master my fear and reconcile the tension I had always felt between my dream of being an inspirational leader and my safety zone. The pain of not making enough money to pay even minimal bills when I loved beauty and luxury led me to attract attention with my message and live abundantly. Pain had forced me to be honest with myself about how far away from my potential self I really was. Pain ignited my desire for change. Watching my husband dance with all these women was exhilarating. I felt as though I had turned a huge corner. What I didn't know was that grief was waiting around the next corner.

CHAPTER 30

PLEASURE IN PAIN

I got an unexpected call from my sister Amy in Australia, and when I heard a crack in her voice, I knew something was wrong. She passed the phone to my dad, who choked back the tears like any strong Aussie male would do and told me Mum had been diagnosed with terminal cancer. She was only 66. I stayed as strong as I could during the conversation, mostly for them. That's what the eldest child does. She takes care of the feelings and needs of the others. I could do that. I can't remember the exact words that Dad spoke that day, but I remember how he felt. Shattered. The woman he had loved with every fiber of his being had been told she only had a few months—possibly weeks—to live. I knew he felt like shouting, "Please have it be me instead. I am supposed to go before her."

I hung up the phone and stared out the window. The rest of the day was merely a blur.

I was in the midst of leading an *Art of Feminine Presence*® teacher training in Austin, Texas. I had to return to a room of women who were expecting me to be their strong leader that morning, but when I shared the news, it was clear I couldn't provide my usual solid presence. Datta took over and taught the speaker training portion earlier than planned. I sat in the back of the room, dazed, looking out the window at trees budding with blossoms. The news had been accompanied by the message no one wants to hear: "This is aggressive, it's spreading fast, and it cannot be treated."

I was on the other side of the world, halfway through a six-day training. My family assured me that I didn't need to leave immediately and fly back to Australia, since it could be months before the cancer reached the final stages. Months! Mum was a healthy, vibrant, smart, wise, loving mum, sister, daughter, teacher, and friend. She'd just retired from teaching and was looking forward eagerly to the next chapter in her life.

She had also been blessed with the birth of her first grandchild, and she loved every minute with my sister Bridget's baby girl, Evelyn. She had started to volunteer at the local hospital; she looked after her friends when they were down; she cared and acted against injustices. Without a full teaching load, she emailed me more often. She didn't only send me emails with details of birthdays and Christmas festivities but of the most important days to her. This email I got from her on February 14th, 2008, sums up her spirit.

Hi there,
Just wanted to share the most wonderful day in Australia. When Kevin Rudd was elected last

year, he said the first thing he would do in government was to say "Sorry" to Australian Aborigines, especially the "Stolen Generations." This happened yesterday. I went into Federation Square in the city to join the throng and watch Parliament on the big screen. It was a most emotional day. I shed tears as most did, and again today as I was describing it all to your brother. Singer, composer Archie Roach, whose mother was taken from her mother and who was brought up in an orphanage, thinking his sister was his mother, sung a song about the children taken away from their families. He received a standing ovation that went on and on and on. He broke down and then just said, "You don't know what this means."

The new government is making a priority of really improving Aboriginal education, health, and life expectancy.

John Howard was the only living Prime Minister not to attend the momentous occasion yesterday. He refused to say 'sorry' for 11 years and some of his cronies, not many, walked out before the main speech.

This has been a great week!

Lots of love

M

After receiving the news about Mum's cancer, my internal "spiritual warrior" kicked in, and I sent a callout to all the world-class healers I knew who could possibly help create a miracle. I believed there is always a way to heal the body given the intention, and I knew Mum would not want her life cut short. She had many trips to faraway lands already scheduled in her mind. I had heard countless stories of others who were told they had a terminal illness and they had gotten better. I was back to feeling better because I was on a mission to get Mum well. I was encouraged to hear she was feeling a lot more energy the day after I asked some remote healers to work on her.

Day Five of the six-day training came, and I still felt shaky. I had been checking in with my family each day, and they reported a steady decline in Mum's health. Dad had just told me that she would probably stay in the hospital now and not go home. That was not the positive news I wanted to hear. *It sounds like the doctors are giving up on her,* I thought with frustration. *They do not believe in what is possible for Mum.* All I knew was that I had to hold it together for one more day.

I walked into the training room after dinner to prepare for the last session. I was met with a soft, slow, nurturing feminine voice that filled the room. I started tuning in to the words of that song and hearing them like I had never heard before:

I am sailing, I am sailing,
home again across the sea.
I am sailing stormy waters
to be near you, to be free.

My legs buckled and I plunged into tears. I knew in that moment that Mum's time was short and her spirit was singing me this beautiful song. In 20 minutes I had to face 50 women, and I literally couldn't stand up on my own. Someone called Datta to come and get me. He peeled me off the floor and carried me out in his arms. I did not teach that night.

I'd never lost someone so close to me before, let alone in such an unexpected way with no time to prepare. I couldn't stop shaking my head. It was the physical representation of being in total shock that this was happening—all in a matter of days. Anytime I thought about what was going on, I found myself shaking my head in disbelief.

The training ended and the next day I woke up in our hotel room in Austin and checked in with my family. We had little time to process what we were doing next and when we were going to see Mum. We had a busy life. Picking up everything to head to Australia would not be the easiest thing for us to do, but we knew we'd be going soon. We just didn't know how soon.

When we got Dad on the line, he said, "You should come home immediately. The doctors have told us that she probably only has a few days left."

How did the prognosis change from giving her a few months to a few weeks to a few days? It made no sense.

We didn't delay. We had our assistant expedite our passports from Colorado, booked an international flight leaving late the following day, and traveled to LA so we had the least amount of flying time to do the next day.

I was woken up early the next morning by my brother Adam on the phone. "Mum just passed away. She was peaceful."

I never got to see her again. It all happened too quickly. I had already shed excruciatingly painful tears over the past few days, so I greeted Adam's news with more of my matter-of-fact personality—at least externally. *Okay, we need to pack, I need to get home to be with my family, and we need to go to the airport.* By ten o'clock that night we were waiting at the Qantas gate in the LA international terminal.

Something drew my attention to the gate lounge opposite us, and I noticed someone who looked a lot like Mum. She had the same dead-straight blonde hair in a bob cut just below her chin, an angular nose, and fair skin that made her look younger than her years. She wore the same cherry red Mum often wore, and she was the spitting image from the side view I had. Then I realized it couldn't be her—it could never be her. I'd never see her again. I sobbed audibly and uncontrollably—in front of 200 people waiting to board, my head in Datta's lap. I am an image-driven person most of the time. I want to be seen as a put-together, stylish, smart, unique, original, mature, and an all-around amazing person. So not caring about what others thought as I shattered into pieces was quite a feat. That's what love does, I guess. It forced me to put aside my ego so I could feel the pain of my heart breaking.

My throat locked up for weeks. I didn't want to take a deep breath. I felt if I breathed deep enough to feel all of the pain, I would end up on the floor again. To step into our Melbourne family home with her not to greet me was unbearable. The sound of my father crying from his bedroom the morning after the funeral broke my heart. To feel so much grief was enough to drive me to drink most nights. I didn't think I could do anything for my family to ease the heartache—until I realized just being with them was soothing, restoring me to some normal sense of myself.

We'd come to Australia only eight weeks before, as we'd been asked out of the blue to speak at an event there. It didn't make logical sense to go all that way for a small occasion, but I knew I was meant to go. I felt that nudge from the Divine that I had to go. It was a great event, but the real reason, I realize now, was to spend my final weeks with Mum. I wish I'd known what was going to happen. I wish I'd gotten the chance to say goodbye. Once she was diagnosed, I didn't even get the chance to speak to her on the phone—she was in too much pain. I emailed her a letter for my sister to read her. She did, but that was it.

Thank you, Grace, for the Divine Breadcrumb that led me back to see and spend time with her eight weeks before. Thank you for giving me the impulse to buy her a bunch of flowers for no reason on my final day of being with her on that unplanned trip. I remember her asking, "What are these for?" I wasn't accustomed to buying flowers for her without an occasion. "No reason," I said. "I'm just so grateful for everything you do for us."

I felt some more relief a few weeks after Mum passed away and we'd returned home to Colorado. In the quietness of meditation, I heard a gentle internal voice ask, "Have you ever experienced the pleasure of grief?" I had felt love when some of the waves of grief hit, but had I felt pleasure? No.

One day I noticed that the wooden birdhouse attached to our home above the back deck had started to fill with twigs. Weeks passed, and the melodic chirping of the little chicks started to ring through the backyard and into the kitchen. I would go out each morning and see Mummy and Daddy fly in and out, bringing food for their young. They would swoop in at rapid speed with such precision in their landing and then depart just as fast to fetch more food. I was proud to play a part in looking after them—sending them good wishes and checking on their well-being.

A few days after the hatching I saw one of the little chick's legs falling out of the nest between the birdhouse and the siding of our house. Somehow the nest inside was pushing the birdhouse out from the side of our house, and it created a gap that the leg of the chick had slipped through. I assessed the situation and tried to work out how I could stick this bird's leg back in. I remembered hearing that you shouldn't touch a bird with your hands, as that would leave a scent on them and might cause their parents to abandon them. So I covered my hands with a paper towel and used it to give the birdie's leg a platform for it to step back into the nest. After a few minutes, working together, the bird and I won the battle with gravity. It was back in its nest. My pride grew. I was helping this bird family. I assessed the situation some more and placed some straw and twigs so the bird's legs couldn't fall out. Off I went to work.

When I got home that afternoon, I rushed to the back door to peer through the glass. No legs were hanging out the side. *Yay!* I opened the door to the deck and took in the daylight savings sun, still high in the sky. I didn't notice right away, but it was so quiet outside. It finally dawned on me that I wasn't hearing any sweet melodies. Instead, two birds in our tallest apple tree were squawking at the top of their lungs. I tried to figure out what had happened. Then I looked down, and below the birdhouse on my deck, three chicks had fallen to their deaths. I looked back at the mother and father in the apple tree. I could feel their distress. I could feel the broken hearts of those birds.

I've had experiences before of watching larger animals grieve when they are separated from their young, but never with creatures as small as these birds. I came back inside, fixed myself a glass of water, and before I could get two sips down I burst into tears. I watched my body curl up on the chair like I was hovering above it. A familiar sensation overtook me, one that I can only describe as my skin crawling, wanting to escape the body I was in. That was when the voice whispered again, "Have you ever experienced the pleasure of grief?"

I went with it. I felt emotion in every cell in my body. I felt pleasure and pain intertwining and becoming one. I felt appreciation that I could allow such a thing to move me so deeply. I took comfort in the fact that I was not resistant anymore to my feelings. The pain became pleasure.

Later that day, I felt Mum's presence opposite me. She sat right down at the kitchen table. She never did get to visit Colorado. I wished I had the chance to show her the first home that I owned with Datta, and how great I was at decorating it—how well I was doing in my career. I knew she would have been proud, and I wanted that feeling along with her warm hug and her understated smile that was always full of love. I could feel her pride in every corner of that kitchen as we sipped tea together.

People avoid pain and so end up in it. That night I turned to one of my favorite Rumi poems, "The Question":

> One dervish to another,
> "What was your vision of god's presence?"
> I haven't seen anything.
> But for the sake of conversation, I'll tell you
> a story.
> God's presence is there in front of me,
> a fire on the left,
> a lovely stream on the right.
> One group walks toward the fire, into the fire,
> another toward the sweet flowing water.
> No one knows which are blessed
> and which not.
> Whoever walks into the fire
> appears suddenly in the stream.
> A head goes under on the water surface,
> that head pokes out of the fire.
> Most people guard against going into the fire,
> and so end up in it.
> Those who love the water of pleasure

and make it their devotion
are cheated with this reversal.
The trickery goes further.
The voice of the fire tells the truth, saying
"I am not fire. I am fountainhead.
Come into me and don't mind the sparks."
If you are a friend of God,
fire is your water.
You should wish to have
a hundred thousand sets of moth wings,
so you could burn them away, one set a night.
The moth sees light
and goes into fire.
You should see fire
and go toward light.
Fire is what of God is world-consuming.
Water, world-protecting.
Somehow each gives the appearance of the other.
To these eyes you have now,
what looks like water burns.
What looks like fire
is a great relief to be inside.

I occasionally think about people who live stressful and unhappy lives. Their way to escape may be to take vacations by the
beach, partying, immersing themselves in sports on television,
buying things they don't need, or doing whatever will bring

them instant pleasure. They chase after the water but always end up back in the fire.

The water of pleasure could be a few drinks in the evening. Something habitual and easy instead of facing what is scary but will drive your soul's mission forward.

The water of positivity can look like quickly reframing a negative situation into a positive versus honoring the emotion that is present.

It can be the water of "the spiritual bypass," where everything is perfect as long as you just sweep anything ugly under the carpet.

It can be the water of the mind that says, "Power lies in detachment. Don't get too close. Don't go into the messiness with people; they are not as evolved as I."

The water of avoidance could be watching TV so you never have to face that you are not being the person you really want to be.

That water could be always seeking the early romantic stage of a relationship, and when the going gets tough (i.e., when you get triggered by the other person) you think it's just not meant to be—this person is clearly not your soul mate.

The water moments of relaxation, nurturing, and freedom are important, but if one thinks that is the only place where Grace resides, they are mistaken. God resides everywhere—in hardship and celebration, in birth and death.

God is in the water and the fire, even in those dark corners where you don't want to look. Grace is the light that shines into the darkness and makes the moment beautiful. I have appreciated becoming more masterful in seeing God everywhere, even in grief.

I've appreciated the Divine Breadcrumbs leading me to my ultimate path of joy, discovery, and expansion. Most times, the way they led me was through the fire.

FEEL IT TO HEAL IT

A few years after beginning the *Art of Feminine Presence*®, my Divine inner voice started to nudge me to do some more training in the Enneagram through the Helen Palmer and David Daniels organization. I had been studying the Enneagram since 2002, after I first arrived in Ashland, but I was ready to go deeper. The Enneagram in the Narrative Tradition focuses on the same three critical aspects of self-development as the Art of Feminine Presence®: Psychological, Spiritual, and Somatic.

When we work on these three areas together, the awakening process is accelerated. When someone brings awareness to their psychology, this can loosen the grip of mental and emotional patterns that cause suffering in the mind. When someone brings awareness to their spiritual nature, they increase their capacity to be receptive to the Divine and its guidance. When someone brings awareness to somatic movement, which includes perceiving the body from within, they can loosen the grip that their personality has on their behavior. Instead of behaviors running just on instinct, one will start to make more conscious choices about how to respond to an event.

I arrived at the San Francisco Enneagram workshop excited to do more of my own inner work and not stand at the front of the room for a change. It was held in what looked like an old monastery. My sleeping chamber had just enough room for a single bed and a foot on each side. I had to watch not to scrape my hip on the side of the basin trying to enter the tiny bathroom attached to the bedroom. I didn't care. I've always liked going somewhere different, especially if I could learn something new.

I love what's known as the Narrative Tradition way of learning the Enneagram. It helps us understand what keeps people stuck in the prison of their mind, emotions, and habitual actions. They learn to talk about themselves in a very open way. This tradition created what is called "Enneagram Panels." People who have the same Enneagram Type sit in front of other students and answer a series of questions for the purpose of revealing their internal landscape so the rest of the group can get a clearer sense of their higher qualities, greatest fears, motivations, and patterns of behavior. This would naturally elicit an abundance of compassion.

There are nine different Enneagram Types, and they all get stuck in different ways. There are nine different lenses that people look at life and other people through, and though we all use all nine according to time and circumstance, each of us has one that we fixate on and use predominantly over the other eight. I loved learning about Datta's lens and my family members' lenses, which made my relationships a lot easier because I stopped thinking they should see things through my lens. What a concept!

I was invited to be part of the Type 4 panel on the second day of the training. I took one of the five chairs at the front of the room.

"How do you know that you are a four?" David Daniels asked me and my fellow Type 4 panelists.

That question was easy, so I reached for the microphone and jumped in. "I know I'm a Type 4 because I am an emotional creature. Not just any type of emotional creature, but one who feels very deeply, who can cry very easily, who can be moved by art intensely, and who enjoys feeling the entire range of emotions and can feel the sweetness in almost all them. Since starting high school I have always tried to find ways to stand out as unique or different. I accomplished that with crazy hairdos and dressing differently from everyone else. I even had a go at being the class clown for a couple of years, which worked well, too."

The audience chuckled. Like usual, once I got going in front of an audience, it was hard to stop me. I let the laughter have its space and continued.

"Being authentic, having a deep emotional connection with others, and not being superficial were all crucial to me in my teens and twenties. I have always been a romantic and an idealist, prone to seeing what is missing rather than what I have already. The grass seemed to always be greener in someone else's pasture."

Others on the panel answered the question in their own ways. We all had a good laugh at ourselves because Type 4s are known to be more dramatic than most, so we enjoyed putting on a show for everyone. The audience clearly appreciated the entertainment value. More questions were thrown at us, which we handled with ease. I felt I had a firm grasp on how to answer most of those questions, like a good and helpful exemplar should. Then the question that had always confused me popped up.

"What is your relationship to feeling abandoned?" David spoke into the microphone. "Enneagram Type 4s usually have a significant experience of abandonment by someone very close to them early on in life. This disconnection of what the young person feels is an idealized love they experienced with someone, and it kick-starts their ego to fixate on finding that ideal love or ideal situation again. It also kick-starts a pattern of feeling abandoned."

I had never related to abandonment in my childhood. My parents didn't abandon me. They were not even close to the type of parents who would withdraw love, so how did I experience abandonment? I didn't understand it. I had weekly nightmares of Datta leaving me, but I thought that was normal.

As David put the question into context, I heard his words loud and clear, "Sometimes it's not a family member but a best friend who leaves..."

That was enough to spark spontaneous memories that flooded back to me as David kept talking. My hands became clammy and my heart pounded. I had fainted a few times before in my life, so I knew what was about to come. In about ninety seconds or less, I would fall off my chair and hit the floor sideways—creating serious entertainment value.

Oh no, it's going to happen right now in front of all these people and there is nothing I can do about it. I focused on my bright red toenails and my breathing. I tried not to think of anything, but I saw in full color a constant reel of memories of my best friend in primary school playing with me.

Candice and I both loved to sing and dance, jump rope, and get good grades. We were both "Goodie Two-shoes." We were both smart kids. Candice was super smart. These days she is an actuary, which in simple terms means she's super freaking smart. We met on the first day of primary school when we were told to line up on the blue dots on the asphalt playground. She was the first one to introduce herself to me. I had never seen someone with skin that dark or hair that black. Her Indian features were stunning to my five-year-old eyes. We clicked. We were as close as best friends could get. We were inseparable until our final year of primary school.

Two scenes were now playing at the same time. In one view, the panel beside me were laughing and sharing, and I couldn't figure out if anyone in the 40-person audience had seen my clammy hands or paler-than-usual face. In the other view unfolded how Candice and I were separated.

One day near the end of the school year, the teacher read out all the names going into Mrs. Sandham's final year class. My name echoed across the classroom along with 28 others. Candice's wasn't on the list. She was put into a different class. I was disappointed but not devastated that day. I would be separated from many other people in my class, and we would still play together every recess and lunch and after school and on the weekends.

In the next scene Candice skipped off happily and became new best friends with a sweet girl named Corina. Corina was smarter than me. Corina had darker skin and was far more exotic than me. Within weeks of starting final year, they became inseparable. I could play with them, and I did, but I was clearly not her best friend anymore. I, on the other hand, did not find a new best friend to replace Candice. I had some friends that lasted a few months or a year, but I was lonely because I didn't have my own special person from age ten all the way to sixteen.

The night before most school years began from then on, I cried myself to sleep. Some years the feeling of not having a best friend was so bad, I begged Mum to let me miss the first day, which of course she never let me do.

The wound of being abandoned by my best friend and losing the most precious friendship I'd ever had buried itself deep in my psyche. I had completely forgotten about it. I had thought it was just a small loss that happened at the end of Grade 5.

"Um, I need to share something," I interrupted as my awareness came back into the room. I looked at David. "I'm feeling very light-headed. I'm processing a memory that is just coming back, and I might need to lie down in a moment for safety. I might pass out."

"Well, I think we are done anyhow," David said. "Let's thank the panel."

I kept breathing and focusing on my two big toes peering out of my sandals. Once the applause ended, I rushed straight to my room and had one of the most cathartic releases of my life under the wooden cross hanging above my bed. I didn't know when it was going to end. I didn't know who could hear me through the paper-thin walls. I lay there with that little girl inside me howling, her innocent body rocking back and forth inside mine for over an hour. As soon as I thought she was done, she had more to be released. This little girl was abandoned. She was not able to feel connected with anyone until she reached her final year of high school, when she became best friends with Fiona.

On that day in the San Francisco training room, the audience was made up of 30 therapists, 10 coaches, and other masters of the Enneagram with decades of experience. They held a safe space for a forgotten and repressed memory to surface. I had to feel it to heal it. I was reminded that everyone's soul knows the right time to remember and heal past trauma. In a room as mature and competent as this, the memory surfaced. I was also reminded of the power of the body's ability to store and release memories. I viscerally experienced the language of the unconscious, and the more I did embodiment work, the more would come to the surface to be healed. I could see when the pattern of abandonment started, and that it wasn't my fault. I could see where my fixation for ideal love started.

When I returned to the training room a few hours later, David approached me to see how I was. I shared how surprised I was by the intensity of the memory.

He offered, "Memories will come back to serve you some-times. They may be difficult to process. It might be a strong rush of energy with that memory. The memory might be painful, but it is coming out of the dark to have the light transmute it. Don't fear the rush of energy. These come up only when there is a place for them to come up."

On my flight home to Colorado, I remembered the movie *The Prince of Tides*. Barbara Streisand's character was a thera-pist who started working with a resistant, sarcastic man played by Nick Nolte. He didn't remember some horrific experiences that happened in his childhood. He had blocked them out as a coping mechanism, and all his relationships were suffering but he didn't know why. In the safety of the relationship and over many therapy sessions the memory came back, and the final release of that memory freed him. That release gave him back his life and marriage. I wrote down my surprise experience in my journal before I hit the tarmac and underlined my last sentence twice: You have to feel it to heal it.

Since that day I have felt much more freedom and much less fear of rejection. The nightmares of Datta leaving me have subsided and our love keeps growing stronger. The positive impact I've been able to have through my work grows each year because I don't have the brakes on anymore. The woman full of fear has turned into a woman who doesn't think about being brave, and instead takes risks that pay off. I am in the fittest shape of my life. I have friends who support me, and I am one of the happiest people I know.

This experience at the Enneagram training was another reminder that to live in the coolness and pleasure of the water is nice, but sometimes you must to go into the fire to turn those stuck memories into beautiful sparks.

• C H A P T E R   3 2 •

PERFECTION

I hadn't been back to Ashland in six years. Datta had returned several times to see his boys and put on speaking workshops, but I was busy building our business and getting some much-needed alone time. When we received the joyous news of Datta's oldest son Deva's engagement to his sweetheart, we both looked forward to spending a few days there for the wedding. Given the transient nature of Ashland, many of my closest friends had also moved since we had. I had two friends I wanted to make sure I saw, so I set up a time for me to meet them at the café upstairs in Bloomsbury Books. It had remained my favorite tea spot, especially since that's where Datta and I held our first meeting about playing music together. I loved that they still sold the same brand of tea on the counter and the same type of scones were on display behind the glass.

I'm a one-on-one kind of gal, so I met my first friend at one and the other at two-thirty so we could have quality time together. So much time had passed, I felt like a different woman.

I tried not to be embarrassed for the young woman I used to be and was proud I could share how things were going so well—personally and professionally. As it got close to four o'clock, we packed up our things, bussed our table, and I said goodbye to my friend. She headed to the back door that exited to the patio and parking lot and I to the front stairs that led down to the bookstore.

As I walked toward the front, I turned my head slightly to the right. Sitting at the front corner table—by himself—was Robert. He was wearing a red baseball cap while focusing on his computer, not looking a day older than I saw him last. He had his head buried in concentration, so I had a split second to decide whether to pretend I didn't see him or approach.

"Hi, Robert." I caught him off guard.

"Hi there," he said in his low, gentle voice. "Are you back for a visit? I heard you had left town."

"Yes. Nine years ago now. I'm here for a few days."

"Oh, that's great," he said, trying to think of what he would say next.

I chose to stop because I wanted to see how he was, but more so I wanted him to see me looking hot, happy, slim—and with a diamond ring on my finger. Yes, I wanted him to know what he was missing.

"You look fantastic," he said.

I didn't sit down, because I didn't want to engage too much. I just wanted this moment to be part of my story somehow. Maybe some final confirmation of sorts. I tried to stay centered as I started to blush. A feeling of rejection still lingered, one that maybe I will always have, but that ring on my finger and knowing that I was having a great hair day got me through.

"How have you been?" I asked.

"I've been doing well. Not a whole lot has changed."

He never gave too much away. That seemed more irritating than cute now. A young girl walked up the stairs from the bookstore and sat down next to him. "This is Sophia." His daughter was blonde and looked like the perfect mix of him and Rachael. She was 13.

She said a quick, uninterested "Hi" and picked up a felt pen and started to write on a pad of paper. As he interacted with her, I realized I had no animosity toward him, only gratitude for the part he unknowingly played in my life. I saw a man who was part of a lost society—a society in love with love and freedom but detached from the ability to sustain a committed relationship. Many of these people found their way to Ashland.

"I'll leave you both to it. Great to see you, Robert," I said.

He looked up and said with a sincerity that surprised me, "I'm happy that you are happy."

I found myself responding before I could censor myself, "Thank you for being a big part of me being here. You've been a gift in my life."

He smiled, and I could tell he didn't know how to respond.

"See you later," I said confidently, flicking my long, freshly washed hair over my shoulder and turning away from him.

I walked down the wide staircase onto the main floor of the bookstore feeling my heart beating a little faster than usual. I also felt a sense of completion. *Feeling great about your life is the sweetest victory,* I thought.

As I do every time I enter a bookstore, I found the Psychology, Spirituality, and Self-Help section. I scanned the many best-selling authors and teachers on that shelf. Some I'd had the pleasure to meet and work with during my time in Ashland. Some were living far from the message they espoused, and some were the most wise and humble people I've met. *It's an interesting industry we're in,* I thought. Image plays a big part.

All the books in the *Conversations with God* series were lined up on the shelf, and I couldn't help envisioning that one day my books would form their own row.

I looked down at my watch. It was time.

I walked outside and found Datta walking up the sidewalk by himself, right on time to pick me up. He seemed to be dancing because of his buoyancy and the positive way he approaches life.

"Did you have a good meeting with your friends?" he asked.

"I sure did. It was perfect timing that I got to see them all."

"That's wonderful, beautiful woman of mine." He gave me a passionate kiss on Main Street and took my hand. The strength and power of his hand around mine made me proud.

I was proud to stand beside my bodyguard, nurturer, goofy comedian, and lover. I was proud that I attracted such a perfect man for me. I was proud that I was finally the one chosen.

Hand in hand with my committed man, we walked a street I had gone down hundreds of times on my own. The summer sun made a slow descent behind the peaks of the Siskiyou Mountains. A delicious smell of fresh bread wafted from the bakery. I felt the deepest sense that all was right with the world.

I knew without a doubt that everything was unfolding for me in the most perfect and divine way possible—as it had been all along.

SOUL'S ROAD

The breeze at dawn has secrets to tell you.
Don't go back to sleep.
You must ask for what you really want
Don't go back to sleep
People are going back and forth across the door-
sill where two worlds touch.
The door is round and open.
Don't go back to sleep.
~ **RUMI**

As I read my own story, I realize more than ever before that I've always been led. When I asked for guidance—and even when I didn't—it was always there. When I wanted to figure out how to meet my perfect partner, how to get a work visa to the States, and even which city to move to, the road appeared ahead of me. Did I make the journey more complicated than it needed to be? Perhaps. But sometimes the indirect route is the best way to get to where we want to be. It's all about the learning experiences we need along the way.

Could life be that simple—to just open up, don't resist, and let the road take you somewhere? It is that simple and it's not. It's simple because we have the choice to surrender to the Divine part of ourselves—in every moment. It's not simple because we have our psychology, ego, history, and fears all wound up in a knot that keeps us from letting go of control. That knot can take a lifetime to untangle, but it's the most important work we can ever do.

It was no accident that I started watching *Oprah* the year she began bringing on spiritual teachers as guests. You couldn't pry me away from the TV or stop me cutting classes to watch her. It was no accident the *Seat of the Soul* and *Conversations with God* became the books that I devoured right before I was invited to visit Ashland, where both authors lived. It was no accident that I felt such a strong impulse to give up my singing career and move into the personal and spiritual development arena. When I lined up with that Divine part of myself, I was shown the most magical way to create what I wanted. When I look back on all the serendipitous rendezvous when I first arrived in Ashland, I think to myself, *I couldn't make this up if I tried.*

The road to liberation, love, and fulfillment beyond your wildest dreams has already been created. It's a specific road just for you. Your Higher Self has chosen this road. Let's call it your Soul's Road. The excavation has been done, the gravel has been packed, and many amazing sights have been placed along the way for you to see and experience during your journey. Your Soul knows where it wants to go and what it wants to experience. It has given you all the maps and they have been put in a GPS. You've already started down that road.

On this road you'll arrive at your destination, and as you pull up to the beauty and majesty of that place, suddenly the road will shoot off into the distance and you can see many miles ahead of you. Now there is a new destination. When you arrive there, the same thing happens again. The road shoots out ahead of you. You are never complete, always expanding, and there is always more abundance and growth to experience.

I was on my Soul's Road, being guided, but I veered off. I chose a different GPS to follow. I chose my "Small-Minded Thinking GPS" and not my "Higher Self GPS." At times I felt my strong connection with the Divine and trusted the Higher Self GPS, but I got impatient and let my ego take control of the wheel.

Our small minds only see from a limited viewing place. It cannot see the whole picture. My trip to USA for the first time was an example of that. I thought I would find a music city and continue my music career. I couldn't see the larger picture at the time: that remote, tiny Ashland, Oregon, would be the perfect place for my next home and evolution.

There was no job description for what became my career. There was nowhere I could apply for a job where I could speak to hundreds on stage, start the seminar singing with an opening act, and then move into using all of my intuitive gifts to transform the psyche and spirit of people—and do it traveling to various countries each year with the love of my life.

My small, limited mind thought I should be a singer and study psychology and spiritual development on the side.

My small, limited mind continued on its impatient plight. I'm ready for my big love now! Where is he?

I see impatience everywhere these days. You can do everything you can, but at some point you need to let go of the attachment to timing. Our small, limited minds can't see the entire road ahead yet. Other things may need to unfold before everything on our journey can line up.

Be patient.

I still have to remind myself at times: enjoy the ride and stop acting like a kid in the back seat, saying every few minutes, "Mummy, Daddy, are we there yet?"

I've taken a few detours from the road that my soul has laid for me, but something always put me back on track.

There is no detour we can't find our way around. There is no exit that leads us off our path forever. Even if you crash, that's okay. Your soul is crash-proof. It can't be damaged. Stopping is often the path of least resistance for our souls to get us back on track. Many people crash, and because of the crash they stay in the ditch on the side of the road. They complain they are in the ditch, they go to therapy about being in the ditch, and they continue to live in that ditch without realizing they can just find their way back to their Soul's Road.

Don't curse the crashes or the doors that closed—they may be your soul telling you, *Not that direction.* Trust your Higher Self GPS, follow the signs, and trust you will find the right places to stop along the way. It's leading you to something so unbelievably more magnificent than you have ever imagined. You have more connection to infinite wisdom than you can start to fathom. Be open. Listen to that which wants to pull you in another direction—a more interesting, vulnerable, exciting, and probably scarier direction.

Follow the Divine Breadcrumbs.

I pray the lessons in this book will help me not to fall asleep at the wheel again.

The 10 Lessons I learned in my search for true love and enlightenment:

1. Our small, limited minds will never lead us to all we want. Surrender to your Higher Power and the signals that it sends. Those signals are Divine Breadcrumbs.

2. People aren't always the gift you think they'll be, but they are a gift nonetheless. Those people are Divine Breadcrumbs.

3. Follow your intuitive hits, inner voices, and heart's desires. They are all Divine Breadcrumbs.

4. Everything and everyone is connected and co-creating within an energetic matrix, even though we may not see it. There are no accidents.

5. Embracing your Shadow is not optional on your path of spiritual realization if you wish to make progress.

6. When you are not in the flow of your life, your body will tell you.

7. Don't try to recreate moments from the past. Be present as you dream about an even better future.

8. Letting go of resistance is the foundation of healing.

9. Most people guard against going into the fire and so end up in it.

10. There is no crash you cannot recover and learn from.

Rumi's poem "Love Dogs" talks of separation and union with the Divine. When we feel separation, it hurts for a reason. When we ache, it draws us back to the desire for that aligned feeling of being one with our spiritual Source. The cry-out for help, like a dog whining for its master, is the act that returns us home to our power. Ask for help. Pose the questions you want answers to. Become a Love Dog. Give your life to be one of them.

Today, my patience for enlightenment rises and falls. The tide comes in with the sweetest feeling of expansion in my morning meditation, and I want more of that. Where is it? Then I am reminded that seeking for something outside of myself is never the way to find it. The veil of illusion opens more every day. Peace has washed in and cleared me of constant worry about love, money, losing face—or losing everything.

Practicing compassion for those who hurt me is now easier for me to find. I often merge with my deepest longings; I want to burst with love all the time. I want to show the way for many. I want to experience the potential of who I really am. I want to be the most passionate of Love Dogs. I want to give my life to be one of them. Use me! Use me!

Then those thoughts stop. In the stillness I hear that soft, familiar voice whisper, "Relax...relax...don't try so hard."

It makes me giggle.

I don't know where the Divine Breadcrumbs will take me next, but I'm excited to find out. Too much has happened to not stick my head out the window into the joyous breeze, risk a few bugs in my face, and enjoy the ride. I'm grateful for the road my Soul has laid down for me. I celebrate the detours, pit stops, and all the roads that have crossed mine.

I raise a glass to my past, present, and future—and to yours—as I stick my head out the window and howl with pleasure.

• THE END •

RECOMMENDED RESOURCES

ART OF FEMININE PRESENCE®

Weekly Classes, Weekend Intensives, and Teacher Trainings
These in-person events will help you develop a magnetic presence that attracts the attention you want, both personally and professionally. You will feel more comfortable expressing your femininity, sensuality, and receiving positive attention. You will learn how to follow your body's wisdom and "higher guidance" rather than always pushing to make things happen. This is a powerful path to spiritual realization and living your highest vision.

www.ArtofFemininePresence.com

THE AWAKENING (A LIVE 3-DAY EXPERIENCE)

This is for "World Changers" who are ready for massive global impact. Learn how to inspire change and create abundant living by sharing a consciousness-raising message.

www.AwakenYourImpact.com

Speaking Engagements

Rachael Jayne is a dynamic and entertaining speaker and singer. In her presentations, she weaves in tunes people know and love as well as her own original songs. She will customize the perfect presentation for your audience. To have her appear live at your next event,

email support@grooverseminars.com
or call (970) 377-2562

Awaken TV

Receive a free weekly video with a practice on presence, purpose, and practical spirituality. Sign up at the top of Rachael Jayne's website.

www.RachaelJayne.com

Feminine Presence Meditations (CDs or MP3s)

Rachael Jayne Groover leads you through a series of meditative practices that will increase your feminine energy and personal presence immediately. If you find it difficult to meditate sitting on a cushion and quieting your mind, these meditations will reassure you that you can reach profound energetic and empowering states through these feminine modes of meditation.

www.FeminineMeditations.com

ACKNOWLEDGMENTS

My mum's spirit showed up as I started writing the first words of this book. She was so close I could almost hug her. Tears started streaming down my face as I wrote my first hand-written pages. I have the water marks to prove it.

She used to help me with my homework whenever I needed it. We both loved to write. She would love to look over my shoulder and tell me how great I was and then use all the skill she had as a teacher to correct what was needed to make it flawless. She has been with me through the entire writing of this book, guiding me, believing in me, and accepting me.

Thank you, Tom Bird, for being my "Book Whisperer." You challenged me to not write this from my left brain but instead surrender to what wanted to flow through me. Thank you for creating the space to retreat and let the memories flood back and remind me of many things that I needed to remember in order to rise to the next level of my growth.

John Paine, your editing of this book was masterful. Thank you for all your brilliant suggestions and making things flow.

Coleman Barks delivers the most exquisite translations of Rumi that I chose to sprinkle throughout this memoir. If you ever get a chance to see him infusing his huge heart into Rumi's words, go.

To my Groover Seminars team. The support you abundantly offer to help create our massive vision humbles me. Your commitment to your own growth and to the growth of the company inspires me every day. I appreciate the hundreds of times you've gone above and beyond to support this important work. You are like family to us.

Datta Groover. What more can I say? Thank you for being the love of my life, for being my best friend, and for offering your wisdom and editorial support on this project. I fall more deeply in love with you every day.

Finally, a warm thank-you to all those who have broken my heart. It's wider and more accessible because of you.

ABOUT THE AUTHOR

RACHAEL JAYNE GROOVER is an inspirational speaker and leader of an international community of women committed to their own personal and spiritual development as well as supporting that in others. She is the creator of the Art of Feminine Presence® classes and trainings, which are held worldwide. At the fundamental level of all her resources and programs is a core purpose—to accelerate spiritual awareness and raise global consciousness.

Originally from Melbourne, Australia, Rachael Jayne now lives outside Loveland, Colorado, with her husband Datta and dog Dakota.